Literacy as a Civil Right

Studies in the
Postmodern Theory of Education

Joe L. Kincheloe and Shirley R. Steinberg
General Editors

Vol. 316

PETER LANG
New York • Washington, D.C./Baltimore • Bern
Frankfurt am Main • Berlin • Brussels • Vienna • Oxford

Literacy as a Civil Right

Reclaiming Social Justice
in Literacy Teaching and Learning

Stuart Greene, EDITOR

PETER LANG
New York • Washington, D.C./Baltimore • Bern
Frankfurt am Main • Berlin • Brussels • Vienna • Oxford

Library of Congress Cataloging-in-Publication Data

Literacy as a civil right: reclaiming social justice in literacy teaching and learning /
edited by Stuart Greene.
p. cm. — (Counterpoints; v. 316)
Includes bibliographical references and index.
1. Literacy—Social aspects—United States. 2. Minorities—Education—United States.
3. Racism in education—United States. I. Greene, Stuart.
LC151.L4813   302.2'244—dc22   2007000756
ISBN 978-0-8204-8868-4
ISSN 1058-1634

Bibliographic information published by **Die Deutsche Bibliothek**.
Die Deutsche Bibliothek lists this publication in the "Deutsche
Nationalbibliografie"; detailed bibliographic data is available
on the Internet at http://dnb.ddb.de/.

Cover design by Clear Point Designs

The paper in this book meets the guidelines for permanence and durability
of the Committee on Production Guidelines for Book Longevity
of the Council of Library Resources.

© 2008 Peter Lang Publishing, Inc., New York
29 Broadway, 18th floor, New York, NY 10006
www.peterlang.com

Printed in the United States of America

INTRODUCTION:
TEACHING FOR SOCIAL JUSTICE

STUART GREENE

We have labored shoulder-to-shoulder, working to craft, implement, and assess one of the most important changes in American education. And our legacy is the No Child Left Behind Act, which is a liberating and visionary action for our children. It fulfills the promise of our Constitution, the Emancipation Proclamation, and *Brown v. Board of Education*. Because the achievement gap is the civil rights issue of our time, it is as vital to our democracy as are the 1964 Civil Rights Act and the 1965 Voting Rights Act. Historians and other scholars will look back on the No Child Left Behind Act as a necessary, evolutionary step to secure and sustain the rights of all Americans.

> —*Prepared Remarks for Secretary Paige at the*
> *Annual Conference of the National*
> *Alliance of Black School Educators.*

Education is the one realm in which constitutional guarantee of equal opportunity has not been adequate to promote and protect the social equity embedded in the promise of U. S. democracy. While such equality remains an ideal essential to the health of the republic, its manifestation as tangible reality remains—as the title of this book suggests—elusive.

> —*Manuel Goméz, The Elusive Quest for Equality:*
> *150 Years of Chicano/Chicana Education. (p. v)*

Former secretary of Education Rod Paige's words frame the debate about educa-tion in a way that has captured the imagination of many parents, teachers, and scholars. As he observes, "the achievement gap" in education may very well be "the civil rights issue of our time." His words evoke the promise that *Brown v. Board of Education* held for students of African descent, echoing Chief Justice Warren's declaration that education is a "right which must be made available to all on equal terms." Indeed, the *Brown* case serves as an important legal and moral touchstone for talking about equity.

Still, by conflating the "visionary action" of *Brown* with *Brown II*, Paige perpetuates the mythology of the *Brown* decision by ignoring the Court's failure to provide adequate and immediate relief for students of color—in particular, access to quality education and outcomes (Ladson-Billings, 2004a). Instead, the Court envisioned a notion of literacy associated with citizenship, profes-sionalism, and cultural values—what critical race theorists would call "White property"—not access to the kinds of opportunities that would bring about equity (Harris, 1993). As Anderson (2006) maintains, "[t]he *Brown* decision was the product of a contradictory social reform movement that was at once liberal and conservative" (p. 30). Furthermore, as Prendergast (2002) has observed, "literacy researchers have shown that the outcomes that are claimed for both literacy and education do not necessarily result in the opportunities imagined" by legal recourse (p. 208).

Our concern in this book is that framing the debate surrounding under-achievement and low graduation rates as an "achievement gap" oversimplifies the problem African American, Latino/a, Native American, and students of Asian descent experience in schools. Therefore, we seek to reframe the debate, reappropriating the twin notions of civil rights and social justice by focusing on the sociopolitical context of schooling and a history of policy and neglect that limits enfranchisement of minority students to "a dream deferred." The achievement gap is not the problem, and increased testing and standardization are not the solutions to bringing about equity and the entitlements that derive from "due process" and "equal protection under the law." History is a witness to the ways race and privilege have limited the production, distribution, and use of literacy in our schools. Moreover, racism and unfair treatment trump education, so that even the most well-educated find that "our" society throws up roadblocks to employment, health care, and housing. Although the Court ruled to end legalized segregation, it did so by maintaining the status quo of White privilege.

Indeed, research over the years has demonstrated that many of our nation's children have not had equal access to educational resources and outcomes.

In fact, as Goméz (1999) observes earlier, "Education is the one realm in which constitutional guarantee of equal opportunity has not been adequate to promote and protect the social equity embedded in the promise of U. S. democracy" (p. v). Equality remains elusive. To address education as a civil rights issue is especially relevant at a time when school boards have sought to reverse the mandate to desegregate in favor of establishing "neighborhood" schools, when the federal government has called for increased accountability, "standards" and testing, when inflexible tracking segregates minority students within schools, and when citizens have voted to establish "English-only" policies in American classrooms and end affirmative action. These are unfortunate moments in our history when lawmakers have sought to erode the gains underserved groups have made since the civil rights movement.[1]

Reclaiming Social Justice

The chapters in this book, originally presented at a conference sponsored by the National Council of Teachers of English Assembly for Research in 2006, seek to reclaim the notions of civil rights and social justice that have been appropriated by conservatives to explain the goals of increased accountability and testing—in particular, that seek to bridge the chasm between those students with and without social, cultural, economic, and racial advantages (Cochran-Smith, 2004). Yet this move toward educational reform actually masks racist and deficit ideologies that have contributed to the failure of the very students it seeks to help. Such an approach not only favors privileged students who have access to adequate support, but also results in tests that serve as a "gatekeeping function, reflect[ing] the social stratification of language and wealth in the United States" (Baugh, 1999, p. 26).

As Kozol (1991, 2005) has shown, educational opportunities are not distributed equitably and test results reveal this reality. Indeed, a considerable amount of research has demonstrated that "No Child Left Behind" (NCLB) has actually undercut the goals of democracy, equity, and social justice. For example, the curriculum in schools seems to have narrowed to accommodate increased testing and accountability, so that children do not have opportunities to engage in a wide range of literacy practices. Moreover, the ways assessments are used have perpetuated the stratification of our schools by race and class, enforcing both the exclusion and containment of minority students. State and federally mandated testing have already had profound effects on the financing and governance of schools, and what counts as effective teaching.

To reframe the debate, the authors in this volume address the following questions:

- What does it mean to say that education is a civil right?
- What does it mean to teach for social justice?
- What are the implications of seeing teaching as political and intellectual activities?
- What frameworks can help educators understand successful and unsuccessful teaching of poor and privileged White children and children of color?
- What are the implications of linguistic and cultural diversity for school reform and educational equity?

To "reclaim social justice" will entail our resituating social justice in the context of teaching for civic involvement and democracy, documenting the differences in resources and learning opportunities afforded to some students, but not others. Our understanding of social justice is in keeping with Sonia Nieto's (2006) sense that advancing social justice in schools is political "because it's about *power*: who has it, who makes the key decisions that affect people's lives—or not—and who benefits from these decisions." Social justice is also a "quintessentially *democratic* project because it promotes inclusiveness and fairness." Finally, "social justice is about understanding education and access to literacy as *civil rights*"—as access to quality education that meets the learning needs of each child and that provides an equal distribution of material and emotional resources.

Nieto (2006) describes three components of social justice. The first entails providing students with the resources necessary to become more fully human and to learn to their full potential. All students need access to such material resources as books, curriculum, and financial support, so that their families can live with dignity. All students also need access to emotional resources—a belief in their ability and worth; high expectations and rigorous demands; and a discourse and action to confront deficit ideologies about them and their communities. The second urges teachers to draw on the resources, talents, strengths, and "funds of knowledge" (González & Moll, 2005) that students bring to their education. Students need to see their experiences in the materials we teach; in fact, from a Freirean (1973) perspective, students and teachers need to work collaboratively to define relevant problems and texts that are worth exploring and reading (Solorzano & Yasso, 2000). The third requires that teachers create a learning environment that promotes critical thinking and agency for social change, and that views students and teachers as actors in the struggle for social justice.

Our stance toward social justice is also in keeping with Kevin Kumashiro's (2004) use of the phrase "anti-oppressive education." Such a view is "premised on the notion that many commonsense ways of 'reforming education' actually mask the oppressions that need to be challenged. What results is a deep commitment to changing how we think about and engage in many aspects of education, from curriculum and pedagogy, to school culture and activities, to institutional structure and policies." Thus research from a social justice perspective attempts to make visible the hidden agenda of increased accountability, teacher quality, and the structures of schooling and society that maintain power and privilege. Given this understanding, we offer perspectives that blur the line between researcher and activist.

The Demographic Imperative

Our book is motivated by what some educators have called the "demographic imperative" (e.g., Banks, 1995). This phrase describes our own sense that teachers and researchers can play a significant role in transforming structures of inequality and privilege in schools, ensuring that all students have equal access to both resources and outcomes. At the same time, it is important to critique the ideology that explains the consequences of inequality in education, manifested in the achievement gap that separates White students and students of color. Otherwise, we run the risk of perpetuating that ideology, much the way *Brown* failed to address racism as the source of inequality 50 years ago.

As educators, we need to begin with where we are, and literacy is at the center of what many of us do, no matter what we teach (Nieto, 2003). Educators in positions of power need to engage more fully in the process of making race visible, both as a mark of difference and privilege. This entails making explicit the ways in which institutions of schooling and society are implicated in placing minority students in poverty at distinct disadvantages in achieving access to quality education, housing, health care, and employment. "Contrary to the discourse of equity and the common sense that have been constructed around [recent] policies," Pauline Lipman (2004) argues, "they exacerbate existing educational and social inequities and contribute to new ones" (p. 3). Moreover, we need to understand further, the "cultural divide between teachers and their students … complicated by the lack of sustained attention to preparing teachers to teach across lines of ethnicity/race, language, and social class in most teacher education programs" (Zeichner, 2003, p. 493).

State and federally mandated testing harkens back to an earlier period of American education when aptitude testing was used to "support racial hierarchies and constructs" (Moreno, 1999, pp. xvi–xvii) driven by the eugenics movement and redefinitions of Whiteness. The result was the formulation of inflexible curricula and a disproportionate placement of students of Mexican descent in special education classes because of deficits attributed to both language and culture. We know now, as we did at the beginning of the twentieth century, that intelligence and learning are not inert or fixed and that "display" is always contingent upon context. Moreover, there are "multiple components to intelligence" that standardized tests are not designed to capture. Although it is possible to infer some amount of "cognitive competence" when students do well, it is less clear what we can infer when students do not do well—as is the case with many minority students who have for generations been underserved in America's schools (Rose, 2004, p. xxiv). What we might conclude is that achievement—and the achievement gap—has more to say about opportunity and access than anything else. What worries us is that "reform" simply serves the interests of those in power, providing a continuing rationale for the unequal distribution of resources (e.g., good schools, health care, employment, housing, insurance) and the denial of civil rights (e.g., political power).

More than critique and analysis, we need to develop through literacy research and teaching useful and strategic ways to combat racism in its various forms, providing hope for our students whose life chances are limited by current policy. After all, poor and minority people live in a different America than those who are in power, continually living in disproportionate numbers in inner cities, and attending inferior and inadequate primary and secondary schools. Educators, alone, cannot transform schools, but they can enter into a collective struggle with parents, communities, and students to create social justice.

Current Reform Movements: Creating a Two-Tiered System of Education through Increased Accountability and Testing

African American children, Hispanics, and Native Americans currently score lower than European Americans on vocabulary, reading, writing, and

mathematics tests, as well as on tests that claim to measure scholastic aptitude and intelligence (e.g., Jencks & Phillips, 1998; National Center for
Education Statistics, 2002, 2003). Research not only demonstrates key flaws
in the assumptions used to justify high-stakes testing and accountability
as remedies to the achievement gap (Orfield & Kornhaber, 2001) but also
indicates that such an approach to achieving equity has the potential to
harm the very students that policy has sought to help. Natriello and Pallas's
(2001) review of outcomes in three different states shows the "ethnic/racial"
disparities in performance in Texas, New York, and Minnesota, concluding
that "we should be concerned about their [high-stakes testing] potential
to exacerbate already substantial inequities in schooling" (p. 37). In fact,
Natriello and Pallas argue that one could predict the number of students
who would receive a Regents diploma in New York by examining those
schools with the lowest proportion of minority students and students living
in poverty. The greater the proportion of students of color in a class or those
receiving a free lunch in 1995–1996, the chances of students who receive a
Regents diploma is diminished.

Under scrutiny are schools in low-income minority communities. This
is social discipline directed at mostly Latino and African American schools,
teachers, and communities; implicit in increased testing and accountability
is that these schools, in particular, need to be "regulated" and "disciplined"
(Lipman, 2004, pp. 46–47). However, within a climate of racism, anti-immigrant sentiment, and English-only politics, we need to keep in mind that the
role of schools is to teach students to think and participate in their country's
future—not simply to learn standards (Valdés, 2001). Unfortunately, increased
testing has resulted in a reductive curriculum that focuses language learning
on phonemic awareness and skills, preventing students from developing a
repertoire of strategies for increasing their abilities to comprehend, interpret,
and produce texts of their own.

In fact, we argue that as long as low-income, minority schools are defined
by the low-level skills required to succeed on standardized tests, the gap will
increase between these schools and those serving middle-class White students. As Lipman (2004) observes, students immersed in a culture of testing
will learn that "education is about discrete skills, measurable results, externally validated right answers, and test scores" (p. 81). Moreover, she points
out that "[i]f the new policies reinforce a narrow curriculum and promote
education as test preparation, then students historically denied an opportunity
to learn [will] ... continue to be denied an intellectually powerful education"

that is reserved for those who are more "privileged and immune" to a discourse of accountability (p. 81). In fact, NCLB as a remedy for injustice has the potential to limit students' futures rather than pave the way for opportunity. Using data from the nation's report card, National Assessment of Educational Progress (NAEP), J. Lee (2006) compares post-NCLB (2002–2005) trends in reading and math for fourth and eighth graders with pre-NCLB (1990–2001) trends and concludes that "NCLB has not helped the nation and states significantly narrow the achievement gap. The racial and socioeconomic gap in the NAEP reading and math achievement persists after NCLB" (p. 11). As of 2005, NAEP scores show that the percentage of Black and Latino students performing at or above the Proficient level in mathematics is much lower than their White peers (47% for Whites vs. 13% for Blacks & 19% for Latino/as at grade 4) (J. Lee, 2006).

Similarly, Irvine and Larson's (2001) study of early childhood reading instruction has demonstrated that students are constrained in their use of texts when that instruction focuses on reading as decoding, rather than a social practice that gives students "access to the world" (p. 47). The result of this division is a two-tiered system of education that has significant consequences based on race, ethnicity, and social class. Thus it is less than clear how NCLB can, in former secretary Paige's (2004) words, make schools "more equitable, just, tolerant, and respectful for all students" or how schools can foster students' "personal growth" and "intellectual training." In fact, this two-tiered system of education is a visible manifestation of "White privilege," representing the ways that those in power "hoard" (Brown, et al., 2003) resources and opportunities to serve their own interests.

Given this assumption that White privilege undergirds reform, it is not surprising that Natriello and Pallas (2001) predicted that graduation rates for minority students would fall with increased high-stakes testing. In addition, their concerns have become a reality. According to a recent report (2004) disseminated by the Harvard Civil Rights Project, "Half or more of Black, Hispanic and Native American youth in the United States are getting left behind before high school graduation." The report finds "The national (graduation rate) gap for Blacks is 25 percent; for Hispanics 22 percent; for Native Americans 24 percent. Despite wide ranges within some states, nearly every state shows a large and negative gap between Whites and at least one minority group." Needless to say, the implications of the hidden minority dropout crisis in the United States is far-reaching.

Broadening the Conversation:
Literacy as a Social Practice

At stake in discussions of reform is nothing less than improving the futures of all students, preparing them to think and act critically in an unjust world. Unfortunately, there has been little public debate about how to stem the tide of educational failure in this country. Instead, conservatives have co-opted the conversation about reform, offering to the public the only alternative to solving the problem of persistent failure through accountability and standards. In turn, current policy shifts responsibility from the federal government and the states to individuals and schools; this has occurred despite state and federally mandated policies that have created the very conditions that contribute to lack of resources and achievement in our nation's inner cities (e.g., Lipsitz, 1998). Thus we cannot overlook the inextricable link between what happens in schools, the broader sociopolitical context of school, and our students' life chances.

We see this book as an attempt to broaden the conversation taking place about school reform, unmasking an ideology that maintains unequal relations of power in school and society, reimagining success in schools by understanding the possibilities that grow from a democratic vision of education. Together, the authors in this volume provide an alternative framework to increased testing, offering a more humane vision of education that values agency, rigor, civic responsibility, and democracy. This framework entails seeing literacy as a social practice that involves the ways in which people use texts for culturally meaningful purposes within culturally meaningful activities (e.g., Street, 1995). Language and literacy are tied closely to the ideologies of a culture and, as such, what counts as literacy is associated with historical, cultural, and political values of a community. That literacy is a social practice challenges the assumptions that inform high-stakes testing and the prepackaged literacy programs that teachers have begun to use (Larson, 2001). The false assumption driving current reform is that literacy embodies a set of neutral skills, separate from the ideologies of a culture and its practices.

To view literacy as embodying a set of neutral skills is to ignore Gee's (1996) concept of Discourse as "ways of behaving, interacting, valuing, thinking, believing, and speaking" (pp. xiii–xix) or his observation that to be literate is to successfully negotiate the sometimes conflicting ways of interacting in spaces like school. Standardized tests work against students' own strategies for writing, capturing very little of what students are actually capable. This move is even more significant for children who belong to racial groups that are often positioned on the "wrong side" of the achievement gap.

Organization of the Book

The book has three sections: "The Sociopolitical Context of Schooling," "How Race is Lived in Schools," and "Teaching for Social Justice." These categories are fluid, so that issues in one area will undoubtedly overlap with others. Of particular importance in a book focusing on race and social justice are the prevailing ideological assumptions that inform the racial structure of schools and outcomes. This is the sociopolitical context of schooling that serves as the lens through which we can understand how race is lived in schools.

Informing each section is the view that race is a social construction, a function of how particular racial groups are valued or devalued by society. A serious danger lies in treating race in schools in isolation of a world of struggle that finds its source in law and policy. We use Critical Race Theory (CRT) as both an epistemological and methodological tool in evaluating racism in education in terms of those groups included in the dominant paradigm and those who are not.[2] Specifically, CRT offers new ways to analyze the formation of an ideology that supports and reproduces the current racial structure in the United States and the persistence of social injustices and inequalities in education (Ladson-Billings, 1999; Tate, 1997). A key assumption of CRT is that racism is a permanent feature of the United States that rests on a structural foundation, what Bonilla-Silva (2003) has termed the "racial structure" of a society (p. 37). Since different racial groups receive different social rewards, they each develop different material (and conflicting) interests. Particularly important is an understanding of the frames through which those in power can rationalize social inequality and implement seemingly "race-neutral" policies of increased accountability and standards in education. These policies are part of a "racial ideology" (Bonilla-Silva, 2001) that sustains White privilege "through subtle, institutional and apparently non-racial means" (p. 12). Informed by a commitment to social justice, CRT challenges a dominant ideology and educational practices that are used to subordinate low-income minority students.

Chief among the new methodological tools that CRT provides is narrative: storytelling and counter-storytelling (Ladson-Billings, 2000; Solorzano & Yasso, 2000). One cannot ignore the differential relations of power that come into play when a more dominant worldview comes into conflict with a more subordinate one as is the case when the focus of policy centers on the legitimacy of African American vernacular or Spanish in schools. At the heart of the tension emerging from the stories we tell are questions such as whose story is true and what story will be considered legitimate enough to reach the public? CRT challenges traditional conceptions of story telling and truth, reflecting the multiple and contradictory perspectives from which to understand reality more fully. Such a view constitutes the larger ideological context in which people's stories and frames account for success and failure in schools and for racism in a "colorblind" era of conservative politics (Bonilla-Silva, 2003).

As valuable as studies have been in pointing to the potentially transformative effects CRT can have on teaching (e.g., Lopez & Parker, 2003; see also Ladson-Billings & Tate, 1995; Parker, Deyhle, & Villenas, 1999), little research has focused on how literacy instruction—the ways language in use (e.g., textual interpretations and production of texts)—is both taught and learned in different socioeconomic and racially constructed contexts.

Power and Social Inequality in Schools

The authors in this first section assume that power relations are a fundamental, even unspoken, part of life in schools that are manifested through ability grouping, testing, curriculum, disciplinary policies, pedagogy, and which language to use (Nieto, 2002, p. 57). Policy is a power producing and reproducing political practice that manifests itself in action, words, and deeds (Lipman, 2004, p. 15). Moreover, the sociopolitical context of schooling focuses on the impact of structural inequality based on race, ethnicity, gender, social class, and other differences, challenging accepted notions of success—merit, ambition, talent, and intelligence. Who gets to set educational agendas, how are they defined, and what alternatives are offered? How are we affected materially and ideologically by this racial structure? What are the larger social, economic, and political contexts implicated in different and competing agendas for school reform? To what extent do policies about language literacy support diversity, equity, and social justice?

In Chapter 1, "Still_Black @ the academy.edu: The Challenge of Faculty Racial Identity in Teacher Education," Gloria Ladson-Billings begins to address these questions through the lens of CRT. Here she describes the paradox of teacher education that focuses on diversity and/or social justice and, yet, many such programs rarely have faculty of color in positions of intellectual leadership. Rather, scholars of color in teacher education are given responsibility for dealing with the "diversity" issues while expected to conform to norms of Whiteness that define the terms for engagement in the academy. Using data from a study on African American teacher educators, this chapter looks at the tenuous terms on which scholars of color are allowed to participate in the academy and why these terms thwart the expressed commitments to diversity and social justice institutions purport to embrace.

In Chapter 2, "Education Policy, Race, and Neoliberal Urbanism," Pauline Lipman addresses the centrality of race in neoliberal education policies in the United States, particularly in urban contexts. She examines the relationship of education policy and practice to the political economy and racial politics of neoliberal urbanism. Specifically, she discusses ways in which education accountability, standards, and privatization of schools work to increase educational inequalities and promote the regulation and containment of low-income students of color. She argues that NCLB legislation and other accountability policies lay the groundwork for school choice and other privatization plans, and that these plans are part of gentrification and remaking the city as a space of middle-class stability and Whiteness. In this sense, education policy and practice contribute to racialized structures of power and marginalization in the city. Examining the case study of Chicago, she focuses on education policies and how they are actually lived in schools. Doing so enables her to link macro analyses of global and local, social and economic forces, and lived experiences at the classroom and school level, merging policy analysis and ethnography.

How Race is Lived in Schools

Growing out of our concern for the sociopolitical context of school are the specific ways that race is lived inside schools, how students think about their identities, the racial lessons that the curriculum teaches students, and students' resistance to literacy learning and teaching (e.g., Lewis, 2003; Valdés, 2001). It has become commonplace to think of race as socially constructed and to theorize about the ways that race can help explain differences in achievement. Indeed, race is a social construction that never exists outside of a dominant society's categories. However, this way of posing the problem establishes race as a causal factor, when, as Darder and Torres (2000) point out, the use of the term race has the potential to "conceal the particular set of social conditions experienced by racialized groups that are determined by an interplay of complex social processes, one of which is premised on the articulation of racism to effect legitimate exclusion" (p. 167).

History serves as a constant reminder that the meanings attached to race change quickly, as evidenced by the "racialization" of Mexicans/Mestizos/Afro-Mestizos, resulting from Anglo-Mexican conflicts in the 1840s and 1850s. The important point is that this process of racialization occurred in the "context of dominant ideology, perceived economic interests, and psychological neces-sity [Mexicans were unfit to govern their own land]." Identifying Mexicans as inferior ultimately justified the "expropriation of their lands" (Lopez, 2001). Lipman's (2004) study of schooling in Chicago reveals a similar concern when she describes the demolition of housing projects that once contained low-income minorities to make way for development on what the Chicago Housing Authority believes is valuable property. Moreover, state governments have long classified Mexican children as White to legally segregate them. This has been the case until *Keyes v. School District No. 1* (1973) "called into question the Denver Public Schools' strategy of integrating Mexican American with African American students and calling it desegregation." In this instance, the "Court had to define Mexican Americans as Caucasians and integrate them with African Americans or redefine their ethnic status (as a protected minority group) and integrate them with everyone else" (Donato, 1997, p. 125).

In the final analysis, we argue for the necessity of understanding how students experience school, that is, how their experiences are "shaped by the economic and political limitations that determine the conditions under which students must achieve" (Darder & Torres, 2000, p. 167). Thus this section is motivated by questions such as: what kinds of messages do students give and receive? How is race produced and perpetuated in schools? How do students' racial identities—assigned and chosen—affect their schooling experiences? In what ways is language learning a problem for children who arrive in schools without speaking the language of instruction?

In Chapter 3, "'Even Sweet, Gentle Larry?' The Continuing Significance of Race in Education," Amanda E. Lewis explains that a first step in any conversation about educational equity and diversity, particularly as it applies to racial diversity, is to have a clear understanding of how race is and is not relevant to educational practices and outcomes. A great deal of attention has been given in recent years to the role of race in education. However, she argues that the everydayness of race—the way that race is constructed and negoti-ated in everyday life in schools—has received far too little attention. This has had some important consequences for how the relationship between race and education has been framed in the literature—a central assumption of which is that children come to school, arrive in their classrooms, as "Black" or as "White" or as "Latino" students. What we ignore are the ways these identities get ascribed to them in school and how that ascription process matters for their schooling experiences and outcomes. Though they clearly do not "teach" racial identity in the way they teach multiplication or punctuation, schools are settings where people acquire some version "of the rules of racial classification" and of their own racial identity (Omi & Winant, 1994, p. 60). In the area of educational research, we have not properly understood the reality of what race means for children and others in the context of everyday interaction. Drawing upon ethnographic studies of three classrooms, she illustrates the very processes whereby this happens in schools. Only by taking these realities and their implications seriously can we begin to even imagine much less implement an "education for diversity."

In Chapter 4, "For What It's Worth: Civil Rights and the Price of Literacy," Bob Fecho and Sarah Skinner raise significant questions tied to the themes of this book: what is the price of literacy as a civil right? Is the same tax levied on all and who pays the greatest cost? And to what extent is the access that students have to literacy worth the cost? To answer these questions, Fecho and Skinner focus on one student, Jorge, who was part of a larger study of working-class males that details the ways which students' identities (race and class) are shaped by the school. Jorge's identity formation sheds light on three trends that the authors pinpointed in their larger study: (a) students who embraced literacy often did so at the cost of isolating themselves from their peers; (b) the more these students identified with their peers' culture, the less they acknowledged the role that literacy played in their lives; and (c) the wider the gap between students and the peer group in which they aspired to take part, the more likely students used reading and writing to make sense of their experiences of isolation and exile.

Indeed, some students have easier access to literacy than do others, but few researchers have revealed the costs that some students pay and the ways in which their sacrifices affect their personal constructions of self. Of particular interest to the authors are the ways that students like Jorge and others negotiate the pull of mainstream culture represented by school and students' identification with their families (e.g., their ethnic and linguistic heritage) and peer group culture. Unfortunately, graduate rates indicate that many Latino students opt not to wage the battle that such a negotiation entails. One must ask whether or not schools can play a greater role in supporting students in their attempts to make sense of their lives and to make informed choices about what paths to follow.

In Chapter 5, "The Wages of Whiteness? Literacy and Life Goals in an All-White Suburban High School," Jennifer Seibel Trainor picks up on the economic metaphors that Fecho and Skinner use to complicate notions of White privilege. Specifically, she draws from a yearlong ethnographic study addressing questions of multicultural literacy education and White racism through the stories of several high school seniors and their teacher as they read and wrote about race and identity over the course of the school year. In this project, Trainor focuses on the meanings of White racial identity and attitudes toward race as these are constructed via schooling, in the terms and rhetorical structures of multicultural curricula, and in the cultural practices of literacy. She examines the rhetorical features of students' responses to multicultural texts—the narrative gearshifts, metaphors, and discursive gestures that structure talk and writing about race. She also explores the vectors of influence—textual, pedagogical, social, and institutional—that shape and give rise to these constructions. This chapter draws from the last few months of the school year, as students finished their Senior Projects—a high-stakes multifaceted literacy project required for graduation—and focuses on how White racial identity shapes their acquisition of literacy, and students' access to higher education.

Trainor analyzes multiple perspectives—students, parents, teachers, and administrators—and shows how these perspectives complicate and sometimes contradict the widely held belief that middle-class White students have straightforward access to higher education and the economic and cultural privileges that it confers. This belief derives from a familiar dichotomy that pits privilege, literacy, enfranchisement, and Whiteness on one side, and non-White, disenfranchisement, and illiteracy on the other.

By taking a close look at White students and the "wages" their Whiteness supposedly confers in terms of literacy and access to higher education, she moves us beyond such dichotomies. This up close view allows the dynamic and shifting relationships between literacy, access, and race to come into focus, suggesting that literacy, though it may be White property, as Harris (1993) and Lispsitz (1998) suggest, is contested property, with a market value that is difficult to pin down. Ownership of it is a dynamic process involving rhetorical, curricular, and institutional struggles.

In Chapter 6, "Taming the Beast": Race, Discourse, and Identity in a Middle School Classroom," Adrienne Dixson raises a number of questions that bring into further relief the extent to which literacy is not distributed equitably in low-income urban schools: Who gets to set educational agendas? How are they defined? What alternatives are offered? And how do students' and teachers' understanding of the students' racial identities affect the academic experiences the students have in school with literacy. In her case studies of two classrooms, Dixson demonstrates the ways teachers' assumptions about students' racial identities affect their approaches to teaching, even as these teachers adopt the race-neutral discourse of color blindness. Rather than find ways to build on students' cultural and linguistic resources, the teachers believe that their students' differences are really deficits that limit what their students can learn. Thus, in one class, the teacher limits what students read to those available on tape. In the other class, the teacher restricted students' interactions with one another and ignored students' answers to questions she raised about topics with which students had little interest or background knowledge.

Drawing upon students' counter-narratives, Dixson argues that, for the students in her study, school literacy events were neither relevant nor meaningful for students. This is in contrast to teachers' assertions that they connected instruction to students in culturally meaningful ways, particularly through their choices of what to read with the children. In the end, teachers doled out particular kinds of pedagogies that control and limit what students can know and do. Ultimately, Dixson argues that these pedagogies restrict students' access to literacy, thus helping readers understand the ways in access to literacy is a frustrating endeavor for students of color.

Teaching for Social Justice: Transforming Schools and the Life Chances for Our Students

Given our concern for transforming schools, the authors in this third, and final section, focus on the kinds of teaching and teacher preparation that will increase the life chances of students to become active, critical participants in a democracy, what we call teaching for social justice (e.g., Ball, Ellis, & Wilson, 2004; Ladson-Billings, 1994; Lee, 2001). Here we address the challenges that researchers and teachers for social justice face in the twenty-first century and questions of what language and literacy reform means in diverse communities (Gutiérrez, Baquedano-Lopez, & Alvarez, 2000). Unfortunately, the discourse of testing and accountability has silenced teachers, subordinating their own decision-making processes to scripted lessons (Larson, 2001) to insure that schools will not be placed on probation. Lipman (2004) observes in her study of

Chicago schools that teaching is "so formulaic that they result in mechanical, slow paced lessons, regardless of students' actual understanding" (p. 90). Kozol (2005) describes these lessons as "confections of apartheid," pointing out that the "relentless" use of scripted lessons occurs in low-income schools that serve African American and Latino/a students. Moreover, he states, "no matter by what arguments of urgency or practicality they have been justified, they cannot fail to further deepen the divisions of society" (pp. 78, 86).

Neglected are the culturally relevant approaches to teaching that build on students' sociolinguistic backgrounds and emphasize students' production of knowledge. Teachers are forced to limit student access to fully contextualized writing and critical thinking tasks that build on the social practices of students from various ethnic backgrounds and to limit experimentation with different genres of writing. This narrows classroom opportunities for the kind of literacy education that can bring about life-long learning, civic participation, and democracy that is typically reserved for students whose families live and work within the White power structure. Rather than promoting personal growth or equity, as Paige (2004) describes education, increased testing, and accountability erase differences in an increasingly diverse student population, preparing low-income minority students for low-paying jobs in a growing service economy.

As a consequence, teachers are left with the ethical conflict between providing the literacy educational opportunities they know their students deserve and doing what school administrators are pressuring them to do: provide the type of test-prep curriculum in writing and reading that denies their students' cultural identities, thereby increasing the level of disengagement of their students from their classrooms and schooling in general. Narrowing curriculum options and limiting teachers' creativity and imagination may very well explain why 50% of new teachers from urban schools leave teaching within the first five years of their teaching careers (Education Commission of the States, 2000; Haberman, 1995; Haycock, 1998). Teachers enter the profession with a commitment to contributing to society and helping others (Farkas, Johnson, & Foleno, 2000), but they become disheartened because they do not receive the kind of support that would help them meet these goals (Haberman, 1995; Johnson, 1990).

In Chapter 7, Carol D. Lee addresses these issues, building upon Toni Morrison's metaphor of "playing in the dark" to examine two trends that on the surface appear to be in tension: (a) the obtuse references to race to classify those students who typically most underachieve in U.S. schools (what Lee calls the popular colorization of America), using the changing demographics of the U.S. population as the most prominent warrant for funding particular reforms; and (b) the explicit markers of Blackness in the language and icons of popular culture, including the literary nature of such language. Lee argues for the irony of these two themes coexisting. She posits that in terms of literacy research and practice, a significant resource for the current and persistent achievement gap is ironically in the very cultural practices that are signaled as the source of the problem.

In the final chapter, Kris Gutiérrez argues for a sociocritical literacy as both the means and object of a new language and literacy agenda oriented toward social justice. Examining the politics of race, class, and gender and their proxies—English language proficiency, ability, learning styles, and merit, for example—she demonstrates how "othering" nondominant students is both an institutional and embodied accomplishment facilitated by reductive and discriminatory language and literacy policies. Using critical race and cultural historical theoretic perspectives, she further points to normative paradigms that maintain what she calls "White innocence." Specifically, she examines reductive notions of literacy, and the "sameness as fairness" principle currently operant in educational reform, illustrating how the educational vulnerability of nondominant students is at its core an equity issue. By reframing language and literacy as civil rights, she makes evident the importance of a "sociocritical" literacy and an equity-oriented accountability framework.

The Future of Teacher Education

Now, more than ever before, the public connects the problems of public education to their perception that teachers are underqualified and ineffectual. In large-scale surveys of voters, the highest priority among respondents was improving the quality of teachers (The Public Education Network, 2001). They point to what teachers know and do as the most important influences on what students learn (National Commission on Teaching and America's Future, 1996). Langer (2002) found that student achievement in reading, writing, and language skills among middle and high school students is related to the skills their teachers possess. These skills require teachers to make decisions about their students that are contextualized and culturally aware. However, the new definitions of "highly qualified teaching" mandated by NCLB tie measures of teacher competence to a decontextualized view of content area knowledge.

Such a view assumes a universally accepted definition of "what counts" as knowledge about English as a subject and that this knowledge can be readily assessed through standardized teacher tests.

Similar to the narrowing of literacy curricula that has occurred as a result of increased emphasis on standardized testing of students, this shift toward a decontextualized approach to teaching will limit conceptions of teacher preparation. One unfortunate consequence is to devalue teachers whose social and cultural perspectives inform literacy instruction. Current measures of "highly qualified" teaching fail to recognize this kind of knowledge. As Nieto (2003) concludes, "It seems that teachers' work is valued only for its conspicuous conformity to standards-based accountability plans and test performance" (p. 4).

Without a community of teachers that is robust, fed by various perspectives on the meaning of literacy and schooling processes, teachers have little support for challenging traditional literacy practices and understandings. Indeed, the cultural encapsulation of teachers has implications for student achievement. As Ladson-Billings (1994) argues in her study of successful teachers of African American students, successful teachers must participate in a conception of literacy that is broad and culturally embedded. Teachers need to view themselves as "political beings," who understand that their teaching has sociopolitical effects. Zeichner, Tabachnick, and Densmore (1987) propose that teacher knowledge is developed through socialization processes: the interactive level of the classroom wherein students influence teachers' perceptions of teaching; the institutional level, wherein colleagues, administrators and parents influence teachers' conceptions of their work; and the cultural level, wherein societal discourse about education influence school culture.

The resegregation of America's public schools (Boger & Orfield, 2005; Orfield & Yun, 1999) and a monocultural teaching force that is 90% White limits conversations about literacy education in all three areas where teachers may learn and grow—the classroom, the institution, and the larger community. Without professional communities alive with conversations about literacy learning that span various cultural perspectives, literacy teachers cannot grow in their ability to lead students to forge connections between literacy skills and personal, social, and political transformation.

We do not deny that schools need to provide consistency in what teachers do in their classrooms and that students should be learning some important skills. However, the authors in this volume offer an alternative understanding of what it would mean to teach for equity and social justice. For example, it is important to build on students' race, culture, and language to create academic success, rather than suppressing linguistic and cultural diversity (education does not equal assimilation). Defining a sociocultural view of learning, Halcón (2000) points out that

> teachers need to understand the importance of sociocultural factors …. This means not only that they need to understand the social nature of learning …, but that building on the cultural and linguistic background of students is the best foundation for learning. (p. 68)

This also means seeing difference and diversity as resources for learning, using both "heterogeneity and hybridity" to structure the curriculum, including "hybrid language practices" (Gutiérrez, Asato, Santos, & Gotanda, 2002, p. 335).

The goal here is to help students acquire multiple discourses, in contrast to "more traditional views of literacy as rule-governed, monolingual, and monocultural" (Gutiérrez, Baquedano-Lopez, & Alvarez, 2000, p. 226). Finally, teaching for social justice also confronts structural inequities throughout the curriculum that stand in the way of student achievement; it insures equity by providing all children with intellectually challenging education, including material and human resources; and it entails "unlearning conventional wisdom as well as dismantling policies and practices that are disadvantageous for some students at the expense of others" (Nieto, 2002, p. 42).

We are mindful of Ladson-Billings' (2004b) observation that we should not lose sight of our students' academic needs in advancing our own perceived pedagogical goals. In doing so, we will need to reflect upon, even critique, our own practices of teaching for social justice—what we believe is commonsense—to understand why anti-oppressive education is often difficult to practice (Kumashiro, 2004, p. xxvi). Reflective practice within a framework of anti-oppressive or social justice entails coming to terms with the ways we might be complicit in oppressive teaching that we may have no control over, that our knowledge of teaching is always partial and that our practices are always political. After all, teaching for social justice differs from situation to situation and evolves over time. Thus we offer a dynamic model of teaching that stands in contrast to a static conception of teaching that appears to embrace a "one-size-fits-all" approach.

Preparing teachers to teach for social justice is a political act that places teachers' decision-making capabilities and authority at the center of reform. The standards movement has eroded teachers' authority by providing scripted lessons and shut down debate about curricula. In the face of high-stakes testing and learning standards, teachers committed to social justice are pressured to teach toward these standards and must confront conservative policy makers and school board members who perpetuate certain ways of knowing and doing things in school; they do not support alternative frameworks for teaching and learning that teaching for social justice advocates (Lipman, 2004).

Thus, given the current political climate, we would ask, what are the implications of seeing teaching as political and intellectual activities? What is the role of literacy research in addressing the issues of literacy achievement in relation to social justice? Mike Rose (1995) states that the current discourse about public education is "despairing and dismissive," maintaining that it is "shutting down our civic imagination" (p. 1). Thus, we offer a set of alterative discourses, stories that will inspire meaningful social and political discussions about the ways in which the public views literacy education.

The Audience

We raise the questions we have in an effort to initiate change, doing so through a lens of CRT. Such a theory underscores the need to provide an interdisciplinary approach to teaching and doing research. Therefore, the volume includes a group of writers who are sociologists, teachers of language and literacy, and experts in policy. Together, we also challenge the Black-White binary as a means for understanding the central role that race plays in our understanding of schools and what it means to teach for social justice. One place where this change can begin is in teacher preparation, which Gloria Ladson-Billings addresses in her chapter. We also envision a wider audience that includes researchers who have sought to make race visible in schools in policies and curricula that mask the political nature of schooling. In addition, we hope that teachers will see the value of teaching for social justice by infusing multiculturalism throughout the curricula, insuring that we teach all students to participate in a truly democratic society.

Notes

1. For an analysis of neoconservative critiques of schools at a time of increased student diversity, see Gutiérrez, Baquedano-Lopez, & Alvarez (2000), who argue that increased accountability and testing attempt to "subordinate nondominant groups and eventually eliminate their differences in the pursuit of an ideal uniformity" (p. 215).

2. Critical Race Theory grew out of Critical Legal Studies (CLS), which Matsuda (1991) defined as "The work of progressive legal scholars of color who are attempting to develop a jurisprudence that accounts for the role of racism in American law and that work toward the elimination of racism as part of a larger goal of eliminating all forms of subordination" (p. 1331; cf. Crenshaw, Gotanda, Peller, & Thomas, 1995). Although CRT has often been associated with the ways in which law and education have disenfranchised African Americans (Bell, 1987), it has spawned or influenced a number of different movements (e.g., Critical White Studies, LatCrit), which Vargas (2003) refers to collectively as Critical Race Studies. This body of theory values indigenous and community knowledge, giving legitimacy to the experiences and stories of repressed people. Of importance are such questions as who gets to tell the story and what interests influence the telling of one story or another?

References

Anderson, J. (2006). Still segregated, still unequal: Lessons from up north. *Educational Researcher, 35*, 30–33.

Ball, A., Ellis, P., & Wilson, J. (2004, April). Literacies unleashed. Annual Meeting of the American Educational Research Association. San Diego, CA.

Banks, J. (1995). Multicultural education: Historical development, dimensions, and practice. In J. A. Banks & C. A. M. Banks (Eds.), *Handbook of research on multicultural education* (pp. 3–24). New York: Macmillan.

Baugh, J. (1999). *Out of the mouths of slaves: African American language and educational malpractice.* Austin: University of Texas Press.

Bell, D. (1987). *And we are not saved: The elusive quest for racial justice.* New York: Basic Books.

Boger, J., & Orfield, G. (Eds.). (2005). *School resegregation: Must the south turn back?* Chapel Hill: University of North Carolina Press.

Bonilla-Silva, E. (2001). *White supremacy & racism in the post-civil rights era.* London: Lynne Rienner.

Bonilla-Silva, E. (2003). *Racism without racists: Color-blind racism and the persistence of racial inequality in the United States.* Lanham, MD: Rowman & Littlefield.

Brown v. Board of Education, 347 U.S. 483 (1954).

Brown v. Board of Education II, 349 U.S. 294 (1955).

Brown, M., Carnoy, M., Currie, E., Duster, T., Oppenheimer, D., Shultz, M., & Wellman, D. (2003). *White-washing race: The myth of a colorblind society.* Berkeley: University of California Press.

Cochran-Smith, M. (2004). *Walking the road: Race, diversity, and social justice in teacher education:* New York: Teachers College Press.

Crenshaw, K., Gotanda, N., Peller, G., & Thomas, K. (Eds.). (1995). Introduction. In The Public Education Network *Critical race theory: The key writings that formed the movement* (pp. xiii–xxxii). New York: New Press.

Darder, A., & Torres, R. (2000). Mapping the problematics of "race": A critique of Chicano education discourse. In C. Tejeda, C. Martinez, & A. Leonardo (Eds.), *Charting new terrains: Chican(o)/Latina(o) education* (pp. 161–172). Cresskill, NJ: Hampton Press.

Donato, R. (1997). *The other struggle for equal schools: Mexican Americans during the civil rights movement.* New York: SUNY Press.

Education Commission of the States. (2000). In pursuit of quality teaching: Five key strategies for policymakers. Denver, CO.

Farkas, S., Johnson, J., & Foleno, T. (2000). A sense of calling: Who teaches and why. New York: Public Agenda.

Freire, P. (1973). Pedagogy of the oppressed. New York: Seabury Press.

Gee, J. (1996). Social linguistics and literacies: Ideologies in Discourses. Philadelphia: Falmer.

Goméz, M. (1999). Foreword. In J. Moreno (Ed.), The elusive quest for equality: 150 Years of Chicano/Chicana education (pp. v–xix). Cambridge, MA: Harvard Educational Review.

Gutiérrez, K., Asato, J., Santos, M., & Gotanda, N. (2002). Backlash pedagogy: Language and culture and the politics of reform. Review of Education, Pedagogy, and Cultural Studies, 24, 335–351.

Gutiérrez, K., Baquedano-Lopez, P., & Alvarez, H. (2000). The crisis in Latino education. In C. Tejeda, C. Martinez, & A. Leonardo (Eds.), Charting new terrains: Chican(o)/Latina(o) education (pp. 213–232). Cresskill, NJ: Hampton Press.

Haberman, M. (1995). Star teachers of children of poverty. West Lafayette, IN: Kappa Delta Pi.

Halcón, J. (2000). The best for our children: Critical perspectives on literacy for Latino students. New York: Teachers College Press.

Harris, C. (1993). Whiteness as property. Harvard Law Review, 106, 1709–1791.

Harvard Civil Rights Project, The Urban Institute, Advocates for Children of New York and Results for America Study. (2004). Only 50–50 chance of high school graduation for U.S. minority students. Retrieved February 11, 2005, from http://www.civilrightsproject.harvard.edu/news/pressreleases.php/record_id=45/

Haycock, K. (1998). No more settling for less. Thinking K-16, 4, 3–12.

Irvine, P., & Larson, J. (2001). Literacy packages in practice: Constructing academic disadvantage. In J. Larson (Ed.), Literacy as snake oil: Beyond the quick fix (pp. 45–67). New York: Peter Lang.

Jencks, C., & Phillips, M. (Eds.). (1998). The black-white test score gap. Washington, DC: Brookings Institution.

Johnson, S. M. (1990). Teachers at work: Achieving success in our schools. New York: Basic Books.

Keyes v. School District No. 1, Denver, [Colorado], 413 U.S. 189 (1973).

Kozol, J. (1991). Savage inequalities: Children in America's schools. New York: HarperCollins.

Kozol, J. (2005). The shame of the nation: The restoration of apartheid schooling in America. New York: Crown Publishers.

Kumashiro, K. (2004). Against common sense: Teaching and learning toward social justice. New York: Routledge Falmer.

Ladson-Billings, G. (1994). The dreamkeepers. San Francisco: Jossey-Bass.

Ladson-Billings, G. (1999). Just what is critical race theory and what's it doing in a nice field like education? In L. Parker, D. Deyhle, & S. Villenas (Eds.), Race is ... isn't: Critical race theory and qualitative studies in education (pp. 7–30). Boulder, CO: Westview Press.

Ladson-Billings, G. (2000). Racialized discourses and ethnic epistemologies. In N. Denzin & Y. Lincoln (Eds.), Handbook of qualitative research (2nd ed.) (pp. 257–277). Thousand Oaks, CA: Sage Publications.

Ladson-Billings, G. (2004a). Landing on the wrong note: The price we paid for Brown. Educational Researcher, 33, 3–13.

Ladson-Billings, G. (2004b). Foreword. In K. Kumashiro (Ed.), Against common sense: Teaching and learning toward social justice (pp. xiii–xvi), New York: Routledge Falmer.

Ladson-Billings, G., & Tate, W. F. (1995). Toward a critical race theory of education. *Teachers College Record, 97,* 47–68.

Langer, J. (2002). Beating the odds: Teaching middle and high school students to read and write well. *American Educational Research Journal, 38,* 837–880.

Larson, J. (Ed.). (2001). *Literacy as snake oil: Beyond the quick fix.* New York: Peter Lang.

Lee, C. (2001). Is October Brown Chinese? A cultural modeling activity system for underachieving students. *American Educational Research Journal, 38,* 97–142.

Lee, J. (2006). *Tracking achievement gaps and assessing the impact of NCLB on the gaps: An in-depth look into national and state reading and math outcome trends.* Cambridge, MA: Harvard Civil Rights Project.

Lewis, A. (2003). *Race in the schoolyard: Negotiating the color line in classrooms and communities.* New Brunswick, NJ: Rutgers University Press.

Lipman, P. (2004). *High stakes education: Inequality, globalization, and urban school reform.* New York: Routledge Falmer.

Lipsitz, G. (1998). *The possessive investment in whiteness.* Philadelphia: Temple University Press.

Lopez, I. A. (2001). The social construction of race. In R. Delgado & J. Stefancic (Eds.), *Critical race theory: The cutting edge* (2nd ed., pp. 163–175). Philadelphia: Temple University Press.

Matsuda, M. (1991). Voices of America: Accent, antidiscrimination law, and a jurisprudence for the last reconstruction. *Yale Law Journal, 100,* 1329–1407.

Moreno, J. (Ed.). (1999). *The elusive quest for equality: 150 Years of Chicano/Chicana education.* Cambridge, MA: Harvard Educational Review.

National Center for Education Statistics. (2002). *Digest of education statistics: Elementary and secondary education.* Washington, DC: U.S. Department of Education.

National Center for Education Statistics. (April 2003). *Status and trends in the education of Hispanics.* Washington, DC: U.S. Department of Education.

National Commission on Teaching and America's Future. (1996). *What matters most: Teaching for American's future.* Washington, DC: U.S. Department of Education.

Natriello, G., & Pallas, A. (2001). The development and impact of high-stakes testing. In G. Orfield & M. Kornhaber (Eds.), *Raising standards or raising barriers? Inequality and high stakes testing in public education* (pp. 19–38). New York: Century Foundation Press.

Nieto, S. (2002). *Language, culture, and teaching: Critical perspectives for a new century.* Mahwah, NJ: Lawrence Erlbaum Associates.

Nieto, S. (2003). Afterword. In S. Greene & D. Abt-Perkins (Eds.), *Making race visible: Literacy research for cultural understanding* (pp. 201–205). New York: Teachers College Press.

Nieto, S. (2006). Teaching for social justice in schools: Stories of courage and *corazón.* Paper presented at annual meeting of the National Council of Teachers of English Assembly for Research, Chicago, IL.

Omi, M., & Winant, H. (1994). *Racial formation in the United States: From the 1960s to the 1990s* (2nd ed.). New York: Routledge.

Orfield, G., & Kornhaber, M. (Eds.). (2001). *Raising standards or raising barriers? Inequality and high stakes testing in public education.* New York: Century Foundation Press.

Orfield, G., & Yun, J. T. (1999). *Resegregation in American Schools.* Cambridge, MA: Civil Rights Project at Harvard University.

Paige, R. (2004). Prepared Remarks for Secretary Paige at the Annual Conference of the National Alliance of Black School Educators. Retrieved February 26, 2005, from http://www.ed.gov/news/speeches/2004/11/11182004.html

Prendergast, C. (2002). The economy of literacy: How the Supreme Court stalled the civil rights movement. *Harvard Educational Review, 72*, 206–229.

Public Education Network (2001). *Action for All: The Public's Responsibility for Public Education.* ERIC #: ED453304. Washington, DC.

Rose, M. (1995). *Possible lives: The promise of public education in America.* New York: Penguin Books.

Rose, M. (2004). *The mind at work.* New York: Viking.

Solorzano, D., & Yosso, T. (2000). In C. Tejeda, C. Martinez, & A. Leonardo, A. (Eds.), *Charting new terrains: Chican(o)/Latina(o) education* (pp. 35–65). Cresskill, NJ: Hampton Press.

Solorzano, D., & Yosso, T. (2000). Toward a critical race theory of Chicana and Chicano education. In C. Tejeda, C. Martinez, & A. Leonardo, A. (Eds.), *Charting new terrains: Chican(o)/Latina(o) education* (pp. 35–65). Cresskill, NJ: Hampton Press.

Tate, W. (1997). Critical race theory and education: History, theory, and implications. In M. Apple (Ed.), *Review of Educational Research* (Vol. 22, pp. 195–247). Washington, DC: American Educational Research Association.

Valdés, G. (2001). *Learning and not learning English: Latino students in American schools.* New York: Teachers College Press.

Vargas, S. (2003). Introduction. In G. Lopez & L. Parker (Eds.), *Interrogating racism in qualitative research methodology* (pp. 1–18). New York: Peter Lang.

Zeichner, K. (2003). The adequacies and inadequacies of three current strategies to recruit, prepare, and retain the best teachers for all students. *Teachers College Record, 105*, 490–519.

Zeichner, K., Tabachnick, R., & Densmore, K. (1987). Individual, institutional and cultural influences on the development of teachers' craft knowledge. In J. Calderhead (Ed.), *Exploring teachers' thinking* (pp. 21–59). London: Cassell.

I
THE SOCIOPOLITICAL CONTEXT
OF SCHOOLING

STILL_BLACK @STANFORD.EDU:
A STORY OF BLACK LIFE
IN THE ACADEMY

GLORIA LADSON-BILLINGS

Many scholars have written about the challenges faced by students of color in college and graduate school (DeFour & Hirsch, 1990; Epps, Allen, & Haniff 1991; Feagin, 1996; Willie, 2003). The typical discussion on graduate students of color focuses on ways that the students feel marginalized in seminars and classes, their failure to get adequate mentorship throughout graduate school, the lack of research opportunities, and the lack of networking opportunities that might lead to career advancement. This literature also details experiences of scholars of color with a lack of support for work about which they feel passionate—work that addresses the concerns and problems facing their communities of origin.

This chapter takes a somewhat different turn. It includes the aforementioned challenges but looks more specifically at the identity struggles scholars of color face when they decide to pursue academic life. How does one achieve success in the academy and maintain an identity that reflects the perspectives, values, and culture of the family, relatives, neighborhood, and culture that formed you?

As an African American woman scholar, this is a deeply personal telling. As such it reflects my biases and my worldview. However, as *my* story, there is no other way I can tell it. I attempt to tell the story by highlighting some of my graduate student experiences while necessarily diminishing others. Thus,

I have to say as a disclaimer that I received a topflight education at Stanford University. I believe that having the Stanford imprimatur is important in how people value me as a scholar and accept my scholarship. But, when I was a student, I clearly recognized the tension of trying to get through graduate school successfully with my sense of self intact. I consider those two components essential to my rights as a scholar.

We All Landed on Our Feet

A few years ago, a White friend and colleague who attended graduate school with me invited me to speak at her university. I gladly went to the campus, having teased my friend about never inviting me before. Instead of the usual chain hotel stay, I had the pleasure of staying at her home, and we spent our downtime catching up on each other's lives. As we sipped coffee on her deck that overlooked a golf course she remarked, "Well Gloria, it seems that all of us from Stanford landed on our feet, but none of us has become the super star you are." I was stunned at her perception of me in that way and I rejoined with,

> I am not a super star. I work darn hard to do what I do. But, more importantly all of the White students may have landed on their feet but I have at least three tales of woe about Black graduate students in our cohort.

When I mentioned the names of the three students, she confessed that she did not know them. Our school is not that large, and the fact that she did not recognize them was indicative of the way they were made invisible in the graduate school process.

The first student who came to mind was a bright young man from Philadelphia. Jamal[1] and I laughed easily about how weird we thought the "left coast" was. However, in one of our conversations he asked me solemnly, "Do you ever feel like you're not here?" I wasn't sure if his was an existential question. "What do you mean?" I replied.

> I mean, you know you're physically here but people constantly ignore you. You sit in the class and people say terrible, wrong-headed things about Black children as if you weren't there. And, it doesn't get any better if you try to say something. Then they look right through you and dismiss anything you have to say.

Jamal's comments would be echoed in Delpit's (1988) classic article, "The silenced dialogue: Power and pedagogy in educating other people's children."

I did know how he felt. I had experienced it years ago when I first went to graduate school. Indeed the feeling of alienation and dismissal was so present in my early graduate school experience that I vowed never to return to school. It took me seven years to make up my mind to return. Thus, I came to doctoral studies more prepared for the way that elite institutions regard students in general and Black students in particular. I came with no expectations other than to get through it any way I could. Jamal was expecting the institution to be responsive. I knew it would not be. By the spring quarter, Jamal decided that he could not take much more and returned home. The issue was not that he was not capable of academic work. Today he is a university vice president, one of the several top administrative jobs he has held over the past 20 years. I have seen his photograph in a number of publications lauding his expertise in recruiting and retaining students as well as securing major grants for his university. The issue was that the university we were attending did not see him as capable of such a future, and he felt their lack of expectation acutely.

Jamal's alienation and frustration with graduate school pale when compared with that of another student, Aisha. She and I became fast friends. She too was from the East Coast. However, her academic profile far outshone mine. As an undergraduate she went to an Ivy League school. She completed her master's at Harvard and was now at Stanford. I thought this would be a snap for her. What I did not realize was that since her previous schooling was so close to home, she enjoyed the protection of family and longtime friends as she made her way through her earlier degrees. Now, out on the West Coast she was starting to crumble under the oppressive sense of nothingness that came with being a Black student on a campus that had no way to support her hopes and dreams.

Aisha's challenge came when she started describing her interest to her adviser. Nearly after a year in the program, he insisted that she was not a "good fit" for the program and advised her to search for another program area within the school. She finally landed in a new program area only to hear that her "preparation" was inadequate for it and that she would have to take a series of "foundational" courses to be prepared to do the work. It took Aisha almost 10 years to finish her Ph.D. There were times when she had severe financial problems and had to get teaching jobs so that she could support herself. By the time she completed her program, she was so soured on both academe in general and Stanford in particular. She refuses to have anything to do with anyone or anything associated with the university.

Finally, there was Verna. She was a Bay Area native who I was sure would have a better chance adapting to life on the farm.[2] Verna was a nontraditional student in that she was mother to some adult and teenaged children. Coming back to graduate school was her dream come true. She relished the opportunity to read and study, and debate. She was a woman for whom the life of the mind seemed ideal. She loved her classes despite the fact that she found herself being the lone voice that advocated for Black children and their families in education. She struggled to find an adviser until a renowned scholar who understood culture was hired. This became her lifeline, and she marched proudly beside me at graduation. Today, Verna is teaching elementary school children in one of the state's worst school districts. When I asked her whether this is what she chose to do she said, "No, I came to graduate school to become an academic like everybody else, but nobody helped me find an academic job or helped me market myself." For more than 20 years, Verna has used her Stanford education working at a low-paying, almost dysfunctional school with no hope of or time to make the intellectual contribution she is capable of making.

Although my African American classmates did not "land on their feet," I recall the day I was prepared to face the oldest graduate school ritual—the oral defense. From an anthropological perspective, this is the last hurdle before the novitiate can become a full citizen and is welcomed into the community of scholars. Dissertation orals are shrouded in mystery, and scholarly communities like to keep them that way. Horror stories about oral defenses circulate the halls of graduate schools. The story circulating at Stanford was that of the candidate who fainted in the middle of the oral. That story alone was enough to set many a graduate student on edge.

I remember my dissertation oral as if it were yesterday. First of all I was anxious and upset because I did not get a chance to finish during the summer I planned. One of my committee members insisted that one of my chapters was not ready and he refused to sign off on the dissertation. Unfortunately, I was already up against the summer defense deadline and could not make the necessary changes in time to finish by summer's end. This meant that I had to pay another quarter's "terminal graduate registration"[3] fee. I was not a happy camper coming into the fall quarter.

By the time I calmed down and looked at the questionable chapter in the light of day, I had to admit that what I had turned in was rushed, and the corrections I made did make the chapter stronger and the dissertation better. I turned in my dissertation in the fall and prepared for my oral. I had followed the university's rigid rules and accompanying paperwork. My oral defense was posted on the school's bulletin board and published in the *Stanford Daily*.[4]

I dressed in a conservative blue wool suit and heels and made my way to room 104—the faculty room.

Although the faculty room has gone through a much needed renovation and now sports brightly colored walls, when I was a student it was a dull, stately room with beige walls and a long cherry wood table. The walls were adorned with photographs of the previous and current faculty. Back then that means row after row of (in some cases, dead) White men. I sat in the room at the head of the table and felt a bit like Edith Ann, the Lily Tomlin character who was a five-year-old girl who sat in an oversized chair and whose feet did not quite reach the ground. As I looked up at those photos, I said aloud, "Bet you fellas didn't expect to see me here." I think the very fact that I wasn't supposed to be there propelled me safely through the defense.

It Wasn't the Rapture

One of my early experiences at graduate school happened when I arrived on campus one day and the school seemed especially empty. I wandered into the office and asked one of the secretaries (I have a tendency to get to know secretaries and janitors wherever I work) where everyone was. "Oh," she replied, "They've gone to AERA." "What's AERA?" I asked. "Oh, that's the American Educational Research Association, you know, the professional association." The thing was I did NOT know. "Where is the meeting?" I asked. "San Francisco," she responded. So there I was, a mere 37 miles south of San Francisco, yet I was a million miles away from the culture of the community of scholars in my discipline. It was okay for me to attend classes and pay tuition—perhaps even earn a degree—but I was not a member of this culture. This "Black child left behind" experience made an indelible impression on me. One of the reasons being elected president of AERA was so deeply satisfying—a perfect example of the best revenge is living well. It also is the reason why I work hard to encourage students, particularly students of color, to participate in professional associations.

The fact that no professor mentioned to me that I should be attending the professional association is an example of the kind of invisibility that too many students of color experience in graduate school. In my own courses, I introduce students to professional membership at every level. In the preservice classes, I tell students about organizations such as NCTE, NCSS, NCTM, and ASCD. I point out the advantages of joining as students and how such memberships keep them in touch with the latest developments in the field. In my graduate classes, I urge them to join AERA and attend not only the annual meeting but also other meetings such as the Ethnography Forum at Penn or QUIG at the University of Georgia. Being a part of a culture means participating in it in multiple ways.

For those who might think my "left behind" story is an "isolated incident," I have told this at a variety of places and each time a student of color comes up to me later to report that a very similar thing happened to them. Just a few weeks ago, when we were all gathered at AERA, a colleague of mine telephoned a woman he knew who lived in the Chicago area. She had graduated from a Chicago area school, and he was sure she would attend. When he called, he learned that although she had a Ph.D. in education she had never heard of AERA. "Get down here right now!" my colleague sternly admonished her. In about an hour, she joined us at one of the university receptions and stood marveling at the impressive array of scholars who were assembled. I took her aside and showed her how many of her former faculty and peers were appearing on the annual meeting program. She told me that she was working at a job that she hated at a textbook company and that she did not know how to go about getting an academic job. I stood there thinking, "same story, new location."

Acting White

A few years later, after I educated myself about AERA and professional associations, I found myself driving up to San Francisco where AERA was once again being held. This time I was joining the community of scholars by both going to sessions and giving my own paper. In one of the sessions sponsored by the Research Focus on Black Education Special Interest Group, there was a spirited discussion about Fordham and Ogbu's (1986) notion of "acting White." Briefly, their argument is that Black students downplay their academic achievement because their peer group accuses them of trying to "act White" when they perform well academically. This thesis has received a great amount of attention both in the academic and popular literature. CBS News did a feature on it. One of the most popular magazines in the Black community, *Jet*, did a story on it. Everyone was starting to explain Black school failure using this "Acting White" thesis.

Interestingly, a recent empirical study done by Tyson, Darity, and Castellino (2005) indicated that there was no evidence that high-achieving Black students felt any excessive pressure from less-accomplished peers. Instead, Black high achievers report being encouraged by peers who say things such as, "You're taking AP Chemistry? You must be smart" or "You're taking Physics? Isn't that hard?" But I digress.

Back in the AERA session in which "Acting White" was being discussed, one of the panelists—a Black scholar speaking to a mostly Black audience—says "Well, we are here at AERA. We are presenting scholarly papers. We are using Standard English. Are we acting White?" No one responded to his rhetorical question, but I can tell you that the thought that ran through my mind immediately was, "Yes, we are, for clearly if this forum was something Black people organized it would look a lot different."

However, even as part of a large and sometimes impersonal venue like an AERA meeting, a number of Black (and Brown) scholars have worked hard to transform the way scholarship is conducted, presented, and discussed. Some years ago, a White woman who had been elected president of the association decided to attend a number of the sessions sponsored by the Research Focus on Black Education Special Interest Group. Near the end of the annual meeting she approached me and said, "There are actually two AERAs. The one I have been attending all of these years and the one that Black people are attending. Their AERA is more humane, more courteous, and a lot more fun!" Her comments suggest that even when people of color find themselves in institutional structures they do not control, they work to make those structures conform to what they see as a Black norm.

The paradox of remaining Black in the academy is that many of us are recruited *because* we are Black but admonished for exhibiting any markers of that Blackness. What we wear, how we style our hair, how we speak and interact all are under scrutiny. But it is not merely about what we might call a Black aesthetic; it is also about the nature of our scholarship, teaching, and service. It is about the terms on which the academy wants us to operate. It is about the tentative nature of our citizenship both on the campuses and in the community of scholars writ large. In 2000, I began collecting data for what would become a book (Ladson-Billings, 2005) about the lives of African American teacher educators. In the process of interviewing the participants, I began to see a number of common themes that characterized their experiences in the academy. Thus, I began to see that the experiences I was having were not uncommon or specific to me, but rather a set of experiences shared by other Black faculty. As someone trained in qualitative methods, I understood these commonalities as themes that could serve as useful rubrics for understanding these experiences.

There are three themes that characterize the experiences of Black faculty on predominately White campuses. I refer to the themes as "The diversity expert … except when it matters," "You're not like the others … you just speak for them," and "Your work is too narrow…but really it's too Black (ethnic)" (Ladson-Billings, 2005). In the following text, I briefly describe each of those themes.

The Diversity Expert … Except when it Matters

Most faculty of color have had the experience of being seen as the expert in their department, school, college, or campus regarding issues of diversity. When issues regarding diversity arise, faculty of color are regularly called upon. When a student of color has a problem, they are referred to a faculty member of color. When there are concerns about the content of the curriculum, and it needs to include content about diversity, faculty of color are expected to respond.

However, at the same moment faculty of color are called to address these climate issues, their work on these issues do not count in the currency of the academy. The workshops, the problem solving, committee service, and the additional advising do not count when tenure and promotion committees meet to discuss candidates of color. Despite the amount of time that faculty invest in addressing diversity issues, that investment is not rewarded in the same way other colleagues' committee and programmatic service is. The typical Black faculty member who works hard on diversity issues does this work in addition to all of the other responsibilities that come with being a faculty member.

Award winning scholar Robin D. G. Kelley states in the PBS film *Shattering the Silences*, that as a Black faculty member he is the faculty person who not only Black and Latino students but also many White students seek out.[5] His colleagues have perhaps a half-a-dozen students while he has scores of them. His is a common lament. Like some of my colleagues, I would love to have a small seminar of eight to ten students where we could dig deeply into texts and have long discussions. Unfortunately, I have classes that have always more than 20 students and lack the intimacy of a graduate seminar.

At least four of the seven participants in my study (Ladson-Billings, 2005) have conducted "diversity workshops" for their departments, schools, or institutions. They were charged with educating their colleagues and administrators about dealing with the racial, ethnic, cultural, and linguistic changes that were occurring on their campuses. Similarly, Black faculty often were called upon to be the "public face" of the institution to schools and other community entities.

However, these same scholars have been challenged for doing research that was "too Black." Thus, in the arena in which expertise is most valued in the academy, namely research and publication, Black faculty have been discouraged from pursuing their interests in the education of African Americans.

This academic pigeonholing happens often to African American scholars (and other scholars of color) despite their academic disciplines. Henry Louis Gates and Cornel West are usually called upon to be the public voice of race and all things African American in the United States. However, Gates is an English professor and West is a philosopher and theologian. When have we heard from Gates on Western literature despite the fact that this is his area of expertise? When do the media ask West to comment on the philosophic or religious values of the nation? Similarly, scholars such as Shelby Steele and McWhorter have stepped outside of their respective areas of expertise (i.e., English and linguistics) to become apologists for the right in their attacks of social policies such as affirmative action. Their limited knowledge of the social science is not considered because their assignment to the Black racial category gives them authority to be racial spokesmen.

You're not Like the Others ... You Just Speak for Them

This theme speaks specifically to the exotic perceptions of otherness that come with being a person of color. In filmmaker Spike Lee's *Do the Right Thing*, there is a scene in which the character Pino, who is overtly racist, speaks disparagingly about Black people. Lee's character Mookie calls him on it and reminds him that his favorite entertainers and athletes are African Americans. Pino loves people like Michael Jordan and Michael Jackson. Pino responds by saying, "They're different. They're not really Black." What does it mean to be "really Black?"

It is clear to me that many White colleagues, even those who proudly claim liberal credentials, are uncomfortable with certain people of color. Perhaps the fault line I am referencing is class, but I am uncertain that these colleagues are good judges of the class identifications of people of color. Sometimes that fault line is gender. The White female colleague who insists on forging a relationship with another female faculty member of color is visibly nervous in the presence of a Black male. A third fault line is sometimes age. For some reason young Black people strike fear in the hearts of people.

On a faculty trip around the state to visit various institutions and facilities with which the university has contacts, my colleagues and I walked into a Milwaukee high school. We are greeted by a gregarious 14-year-old Black boy who extends his right hand, smiles, and says in a loud voice, "Hi, my name is Kevin." After repeating this statement nearly three times, one of my White male colleagues from the College of Agriculture slipped behind me and whispered, "Who is that?" I responded, "I guess it's Kevin!" The shock of his palpable fear was juxtaposed to an earlier stop of the group to a maximum-security prison where there was no such fear exhibited. When the African American criminals were locked behind bars, my colleagues seemed less anxious, but once we walked into a school in which young Black men were freely walking the corridors they were visibly upset.

Far too many of our White colleagues treat us as if we have some special insight into Black life and culture and regularly call on us in voyeur-like fashion to give them a peek at this exotic world. We become the tour guides to otherness. However, our colleagues are quick to separate us out from the chaos and disorder they read as that otherness. We are "different," "special," and "role models." I think the 1950s term is "we are a credit to our race." The deconstruction of those notions of "role models" and "credits to our race" reveal the perspective of Black and other faculty of color as worthy of White affirmation. We have arrived. We know how to behave in ways acceptable to the academy.

The selection of African American teacher educators often amounts to searching for academic stars. Much like Karen's (1990) findings on who gets into Harvard, Black faculty who get into the academy (particularly the high-status academy) are seen as a "special" class. The specialness is not merely about one's intellectual acumen or educational pedigree. Rather, it is about a sense of how good a "fit" the Black faculty member has with the current community of scholars. Thus, Black faculty find themselves perceived as "different from the rest" but able to provide a window on the thoughts and feelings of the rest.

Several of the Black faculty in my study commented that during the national spectacle of the O. J. Simpson murder trial they were asked by colleagues and members of their institutional community, "Well, what do Black people think about this trial (or verdict or O. J. Simpson himself)?" Besides being insulting from the standpoint of homogenizing all African Americans into one monolithic mindset, such comments also reflect the failure of White colleagues to enter into genuine relationships with African American colleagues.

Participants in the study also spoke about the sense of being "on display" for their schools, colleges, and departments. Besides being the institution's proxy for affirmative action (that I discussed earlier), the Black faculty member often is being presented to say, "See, s/he is just like us," because of his/her ability to "fit in" the institutional environment. The work of fitting in is stressful and challenging. On campuses where there are few scholars of color, Black faculty members experience an uncomfortable need to demonstrate solidarity with all other scholars of color, even when they may disagree. On one major university campus, the university president learned that the "star" African American scholar was being wooed away by another university. "Well, what do you want?" asked the president. "What can we do to convince you to stay?" The African American scholar calmly and carefully replied, "I want there to be enough Black scholars on this campus that I don't have to like them all!" This scholar succinctly described the perennial dilemma of Black faculty. If one is the only Black scholar in the department and one additional African American scholar is hired, the two often feel compelled to present a united front on a variety of issues so that neither is used against the other in subsequent circumstances. One of the participants in my study was the only African American scholar on a prestigious national panel. When she raised some substantive questions about the direction of the work, she was confronted by a comment that "Professor 'So and So' (another African American) agrees with us." "It's as if there is only one Black mind out there and if you disagree with that, you lose your Black person's card. Interestingly, such cards are bestowed or rescinded by White people!"

Your Work is too Narrow ... But Really it's too Black

This theme represents an ongoing challenge of Black academic life. Although many Black faculty members are recruited to bring "diversity" to their departments, schools, colleges, and universities, they are presumed to come to their academic positions within extant research and scholarship paradigms. Everyone wants to hire the Black faculty who replicates the community's orthodoxy. Black and other scholars who choose to do work that looks at their own racial and cultural groups are perceived to be doing "self-interested" work—as if our White colleagues' work is not self-interested.

Far too many times young scholars of color have contacted me agonizing over the fact that senior colleagues have advised them not to do research tied to their racial or cultural groups. They are told that such research will not be published in top-tier journals and will be read as political or polemic. Thus, the very reason for which scholars of color are purportedly invited into the academy is turned on its head. The paradigmatic shifts that scholars of color attempt to make are often thwarted by a reward system that insists that they remain within traditional boundaries.

One of the participants in my book (Ladson-Billings, 2005) explained that when she was preparing for her tenure review, she spent a lot of time and energy educating the promotion and tenure review committee about the nature of her work and the publication outlets she had chosen for her work.

> I don't know what other people do when they put their tenure files together but I had to get the committee to see that my work was bigger than tenure and promotion. I was going to do this work whether I was a professor or not because it's bigger than an academic exercise. It's about the survival of a people!

This more politicized nature of the work of African American scholars also places them in jeopardy of not receiving tenure. The demand for "objective, neutral" scholarship makes almost no sense to African American teacher educators who are keenly aware of the pitiful educational conditions many African American students endure.

In addition, the possibility of blatant racism exists in the academy. Professor Reginald Clark's celebrated case (see, Shea, 1992) illustrates the lengths to which a faculty will go to deny others entrance into the academy. Clark overheard his colleagues discussing his case while working late in his office one night. The committee's voices carried through the office's ductwork, and what he learned shocked him. Clark had the presence of mind to tape record the conversation in which his colleagues expressed concern about granting tenure to a Black man. Clark was awarded $1.4 million in damages against the university.

Clark's case is important because the public discussion was that his work was inadequate. The private tape-recorded discussion was about the lack of a comfort level that his White colleagues believed existed because of his presence. Little discussion of Clark's book on African American family life and school achievement served as a challenge to deficit paradigm work on African American students and their families. Clark was seeking tenure at an institution that had no African American faculty with tenure, and he brought with him a research agenda specifically focused on African Americans.

All of the participants in my book have a research agenda that addresses the education and culture of people of African descent. Most have been challenged at some time in their career about this focus. One participant pointed out that although she has interests in "multicultural education" her primary focus is on the education of African American students. "More than one colleague, dean, or department chair has commented that I should include more 'multicultural' work because my work will be seen as too narrow. I understand that to mean my work is 'too Black'!"

Not All the News is Bad

It may seem that I have framed this discussion solely as a negative one, but that is not the case. There is a silver lining that cannot be overlooked. First, we must be clear. There are a ton of jobs that are worse than working in the academy. Indeed, most Black scholars are working at jobs that are better than those of 90% of other Black people. Despite our complaints about our work, it occurs in comfortable surroundings with a decent reward structure. It is not about hard or demeaning labor. We don't dig ditches or clean toilets. We have the jobs our families and loved ones are proud to tell their friends and neighbors about.

In my own family, my late father proudly told his supervisors at the college where he served as a custodian that he needed time off to attend my brother's graduation from the University of Pennsylvania's Wharton School of Finance. Several years later he told these same supervisors that I was in graduate school at Stanford. Clearly not believing that a poor Black man from West Philadelphia could have children in these illustrious institutions, one supervisor decided to challenge my father. "Well, what is your daughter studying at Stanford?" My father did not know (or care) that much about what I was pursuing but he was cognizant of Stanford's reputation for cutting-edge research. (Indeed, about the time I attended Stanford the university's primary department was doing linguistic research with a celebrated gorilla named Koko). Clearly chagrined by the supervisor's questions my father remarked, "What difference does it matter about what she's studying? That's a place that can make an ape talk."

But more than the pride of individual accomplishment, Black scholars have a tremendous opportunity to transform the academy into more humane institutions that push our thinking and help us live up to the nation's loftiest ideals. In the 1960s, Black, Latina/o, Asian American, Native American, and women scholars pushed for a rethinking of the academy. Some scholars read that history selectively. Not just a matter of adding courses mimicked the old paradigm. It was about creating new paradigms that transgressed boundaries. These "new studies" combined humanities and social sciences. It asked scholars to consider what it means to know the experience of a people through their art, literature, histories, cultures, and other expressions of peoplehood. These studies also included a sense of critique that allows us to look at existing canons.

The deciphering (King, 2003) work of such studies gives us new ways to make sense of texts and histories. It opens new ways of thinking and conceptualizing. It raises our scholarship as well as that of our colleagues to new heights because we are challenged to move beyond the places we became comfortable a generation ago. We recognize the need to search for new concepts, theories, and methodologies. And we take heart in the belief that we can do this work and see ourselves as Still_Black @Stanford.edu.

Notes

1. This and other personal names in this chapter are pseudonyms.
2. Stanford University was first the farm of Senator Leland Stanford and his wife Jane Lathrop Stanford, hence its nickname "the farm."
3. Terminal graduate registration or TGR was the reduced tuition students paid once they were advanced to candidacy. You were required to pay it every quarter until you graduated. Although it was less than regular tuition, it was still a substantial fee.
4. All dissertation orals were publicly announced at Stanford in the campus newspaper.
5. One of Kelley's former colleagues said to me when he left New York University, "We had no idea he had so many students. Now we are scrambling to get people to advise them."

References

DeFour, D., & Hirsch, B. (1990). The adaptation of black graduate students: A social network approach. *American Journal of Community Psychology, 18*(3), 483–503.

Delpit, L. (1988). The silenced dialogue: Power and pedagogy in educating other people's children. *Harvard Educational Review, 58*(3), 280–298.

Epps, E., Allen, W. R., & Haniff, N. (1991). *College in black and white.* Albany, NY: SUNY Press.

Feagin, J. R. (1996). *The agony of education.* New York: Routledge.

Fordham, S. & Ogbu, J. (1986). Black students' school success: Coping with the burden of "acting white." *Urban Review, 18*(3), 176–206.

Karen, D. (1990). Toward a political-organizational model of gatekeeping: The case of elite colleges. *Sociology of Education, 63*(4), 227–240.

King, J. E. (2003). Culture-centered knowledge: Black studies, curriculum transformation, and social action. In J. A. Banks & C. M. Banks (Eds.), *Handbook of research on multicultural education* (pp. 349–378). San Francisco: Jossey-Bass.

Ladson-Billings, G. (2005). *Beyond the big house: African American educators on teacher education.* New York: Teachers College Press.

Shea, C. (1992, August 5). California Supreme Court upholds big award in tenure bias case. *Chronicle of Higher Education*, A12.

Tyson, K, Darity, W., & Castellino, D. (2005). It's not "a black thing": Understanding the "burden of acting white" and other dilemmas of high achievement. *American Sociological Review*, 70(4), 582–605.

Willie, S. S. (2003). *Acting Black: College, identity and the performance of race*. New York: Routledge.

· 2 ·

EDUCATION POLICY, RACE, AND NEOLIBERAL URBANISM

PAULINE LIPMAN

Images of post-Katrina New Orleans projected on TV screens across the globe captured the intersection of the logics of race and capitalism that drive economic and social policy in the United States. The saga of thousands of stranded and desperate men, women, children, and elderly people forced to rely on their own resources and ingenuity to survive after the hurricane revealed both the government's callous disregard for African American lives and the absence of a social welfare infrastructure for low-income and working-class people. It exposed the sedimented economic and social inequalities that pushed one-third of the population of New Orleans, 80% of whom were African American, below the poverty line *before* the hurricane.[1] In short, the Katrina disaster is a concentrated expression of the social realities of U.S. political economy and racial politics in the era of neoliberalism. By neoliberalism, I mean an ensemble of economic and social policies that promote the primacy of the market and individual self-interest, unrestricted flows of capital, deep reductions in the cost of labor, sharp retrenchment of the public sphere, and withdrawal of government from providing for social welfare. In this chapter, I argue that this context has everything to do with the dominant education policy agenda in the United States and its consequences for students of color in particular.

The federal No Child Left Behind (NCLB) law that is driving education policy in the United States has all the hallmarks of the neoliberal agenda. Its central rationale is that improving education is key to economic productivity. The key provisions are increased accountability, high-stakes tests, standards, choice, and centralized regulation of schools reducing the influence of teachers and communities on what is taught and how it is taught. Opening up public education to competition through privatization and the market is the ultimate neoliberal solution. Vouchers for public school students to attend private schools were included in President Bush's initial NCLB proposal. Although vouchers did not make it into the final bill, the likely failure of schools to meet NCLB goals paves the way for large-scale privatization of public schools. Underlying NCLB, and other state-level (e.g., Texas) and local (e.g., Chicago) policies that were its prototypes is the larger neoliberal economic and social project in the United States.

There is a substantial body of scholarship on neoliberalism and education (e.g., Apple, 2001; Aronowitz & Giroux, 1993; Dale, 1989/1990; Hursh, 2004, 2005; Lauder, Brown, Dillabough, & Halsey, 2006; Lipman & Hursh, in press; Saltman, 2005; Tomlinson, 2005; Whitty, Power, & Halpin, 1999), but here I want to focus on the racialized nature of neoliberal education policies in the United States using Chicago as an example. NCLB purports to put equity at the center by focusing on achievement gaps and setting the goal of "leaving no child behind." However, in this chapter I argue that under the rationale of promoting equity, education accountability policies deny the effects of entrenched structural and ideological racism and intensify racial inequalities. I also argue that the policies are part of a cultural politics of race that demonizes communities of color.

Although the effects of NCLB and other local accountability policies are being documented (e.g., Haney, 2000, 2001, 2003; Hursh, 2005; McNeil, 2000; Neil, Guisbond, & Schaeffer, 2004; Valenzuela, 2005), Chicago Public Schools (CPS) provide an advanced example of the effects of education accountability on a local level. Chicago's 1995 school reform established a system of centralized accountability, high-stakes testing, and sanctions for failure. Here I consider what Chicago's policies have meant for low-income children of color and for educational equity and the implications in the present economic and social context. My discussion is drawn from my research and writing on Chicago over the past eight years (Lipman, 2002, 2003, 2004; Lipman & Haines, in press). I begin by summarizing the political economic context. Then I revisit Chicago's 1995 school reform and examine Chicago's recent reform, Renaissance 2010, as case studies of the broader implications of the accountability regime in education.

Neoliberalism, the Restructured Economy, and the Cultural Politics of Race

To clarify what is at stake with dominant education policies, it is important to sketch out the political economic context. A point of departure is analyses of neoliberalism as developed in the work of Stephen Gill (2003) and David Harvey (2004, 2005), among others. The ideological underpinnings of neoliberalism are grounded in the belief that the unimpeded operation of capitalist free markets is the pathway to economic growth, individual freedom, and the reduction of inequality (Harvey, 2005). In this framework, the best form of government is that which governs least, leaving free reign to the market. In practice, the neoliberal state intervenes on the side of business, or, in Barlow's (2003, pp. 73–74) terms, it is the "private investment state." The neoliberal state enacts policies to deregulate markets and corporations, lower the taxes of business and wealthy individuals, replace support for social welfare with demands for personal responsibility (e.g., for retirement funds, education, health care), and privatize public institutions (e.g., prisons and schools). These policies produce dramatic increases in economic and social inequality and intensified impoverishment and crises in everyday life. In turn, the state must rely increasingly on coercion (surveillance, policing, and prisons) to maintain social order (Gill, 2003; Harvey, 2005; Wacquant, 2001).

Despite the ideology of individual freedom and economic growth through the market economy, Gill (2003), Harvey (2005), Smith (1996), and others show that in practice neoliberalism means the concentration of political and economic power in the hands of the capitalist class (Harvey, 2005). It amounts to a massive transfer of social wealth from middle-class, working-class, and low-income people to the extremely rich.[2] Neoliberal governments and corporations accomplish this in a number of ways: through the radical transformation of collective property into private property, breaking unions and lowering wages and benefits, commodifying everything from peasant lands to natural resources, privatizing public goods and services (from water to education), and using international banking and finance institutions to control national economies through debt and the credit system to appropriate the wealth of working people. These economic and social policies are degrading the living standards and working conditions of millions of people across the globe, dislocating populations, devastating the environment, and producing unfathomable disparities between the profoundly wealthy few and the vast majority of the world's population (see Harvey, 2004, 2005).

Deindustrialization and government and corporate actions to weaken unions and reduce wages and benefits combined with the revolution in information technology to restructure the U.S. labor force over the past 25 years. A September 2006 announcement by the Ford Motor Company that it plans to eliminate more than 70,000 union jobs exemplifies that this radical restructuring is still under way. Today's youth face an economically polarized labor force of high-paid professional workers at one end and low-wage service, retail, and manufacturing workers at the other (Castells, 1989). U.S. Department of Labor data on the 50 largest U.S. cities for 1986–1999 confirm a barbell labor structure with growth in high- and low-paid jobs and a decline in the share of mid-skilled middle-income administrative and skilled production work for which one needs at least a high school diploma (Skinner, 2004). As the production and manipulation of knowledge have become central in the economy, education has become critical in gaining access to good paying jobs, which are the minority of new jobs being created. The greatest job growth is in low-paid service and retail jobs. In 1998, 76% of the jobs with the most growth in Illinois paid less than a livable wage, and 51% of these jobs paid below half a livable wage (National Priorities Project, 1998). In 2004, 29% of Illinois families earned incomes at or lower than 200% of the poverty level (National Priorities Project, 2005).

Race is pivotal in the ideology and effects of neoliberalism in the United States. Neoliberalism is overlaid on, and intersects in particular ways with, the social relationships of each country and its particular history. "In the United States, the 400-year legacy of highly organized, state-sponsored systems of racism have great significance for the ways in which the 'grid' of globalized relationships come into being" (Barlow, 2003, p. 9). The disproportionate impoverishment of people of color that was evident with Hurricane Katrina is a product of sedimented racial oppression and neoliberal economic restructuring. A recent report on racial equity in Illinois produced by the Applied Research Center (ARC, in press) illustrates the increased economic disparities between Whites and people of color. For example, ARC reports that in Illinois in 2002, the median household net worth for people of color was $18,160 compared with $111,750 for Whites, and working-age African Americans and Latinos are twice and three times as likely as Whites to be uninsured.[3] (Undocumented Latinos are five times more likely to be uninsured than Whites.) Between 1980 and 2004, the hourly wage gap in Illinois between White workers and Latino workers widened by 24%, and the gap between Whites and Blacks widened by an astounding 162% (Poverty Summit,

2006). People of color are concentrated in low-wage service jobs, including day labor where immigrants are more than five times as likely as nonimmigrants to be employed (ARC, in press). Meanwhile, many African Americans can find no work at all in the new economy (Barlow, 2003).

The neoliberal agenda has had a profound ideological impact as well, and this agenda is a product of the logics of capitalism and racism. Neoliberalism has induced a sea change in the way we think about the role of government in reducing inequality, ensuring a safety net against impoverishment, unemployment, and poverty in old age, and redistributing some of the social wealth from the rich to the poor. Gains in these areas were the product of post–World War II labor and social movements and the social contract between labor and capital.[4] Reversing them has involved a direct assault on labor, drastic cuts in social services (Harvey, 2005), and cultural politics targeting people of color, women, and gays to justify these policies (Duggan, 2003). In particular, entrenched structures and ideologies of racism provided the fertile soil for what David Harvey (2005) calls the reassertion of class rule. Lisa Duggan (2003) writes,

> During every phase, the construction of neoliberal politics and policy in the U.S. has relied on identity and cultural politics. The politics of race, both overt and covert, have been particularly central to the entire project. But the politics of gender and sexuality have intersected with race and class politics at each stage as well. (p. xii)

Justification for cuts in social programs rely on the construction of people of color as their undeserving recipients, with African Americans painted as lazy and welfare cheats and immigrants as a drain on the economy and a threat to a normative English-speaking "America" (Barlow, 2003). Moreover, as unemployment, impoverishment, and social marginalization intensify, the government increasingly resorts to coercion, especially in low-income communities of color, to maintain social control (Brown, 2003; Gill, 2003; Parenti, 1999; Wacquant, 2001). For example, the ARC (in press) reports that for every Black person in an Illinois college or university, there are 2.5 in prison or on parole. In 2001, Illinois' incarceration rate for Blacks was more than 12 times the rate for Whites. This is made acceptable by demonizing people of color, particularly African Americans. At the same time, Post–Civil Rights racism posits a colorblind society in which race is no longer relevant. The neoliberal discourse of individualism and individual choice has become a justification to replace group rights with individual, case-by-case analyses of discrimination. (see Bonilla-Silva, 2003, for a full discussion of this shift.) This is the context in which accountability-based education policy unfolds.

The High Stakes of Education Accountability: The Chicago Example

In *High Stakes Education* (Lipman, 2004), I describe ways in which seemingly race-neutral education accountability policies in Chicago are highly racialized. I show that they have differential impact by race and ethnicity and reinforce and extend existing forms of exclusion, oppression, and marginalization without seeming to do so. I also suggest that these education policies are grounded in, and contribute to, the cultural construction of communities of color as deficient and in need of social regulation. In this sense education policy works as a power-producing and reproducing social practice that operates on multiple dimensions (Ball, 1994). It is a "text" that sets parameters of actions and goals, and which educators and others "read" and "rewrite" in different ways in specific local contexts. It is also a "discourse"—a set of values, practices, and ways of talking that shape consciousness and teach people certain social identities (Ball).

Chicago's 1995 education reform is well known as an early model of top-down accountability based on high-stakes tests. Thus Chicago serves as an advanced example of what we are beginning to see as these policies become more deeply embedded across the United States. Previewing NCLB since 1995, school officials have put hundreds of the city's schools on probation, mandated the retention of thousands of students who have failed to meet test benchmarks, and closed and restructured "failing" schools. The students and schools subject to these sanctions are almost all African American and Latino. Simultaneously, Chicago has expanded educational "options," for example, public school military academies (in 2006 there were 4 military high schools and 24 military cadet corps middle schools), scripted direct instruction schools, and new vocational high schools—all these options are located almost entirely in African American and Latino neighborhoods. The district also created high-status International Baccalaureate programs and six new highly selective college preparatory magnet high schools. These magnet schools are so selective that approximately 2,000 eighth grade applicants competed for 200 freshmen slots at Northside College Prep when it opened in 1999, and 2,050 applicants competed for 381 slots at the new Walter Payton College Prep the following year (Williams, 2006). Only students with high test scores were even qualified to apply. The vast majority of students, 91% of whom are students of color, attend neighborhood elementary and high schools and many of the latter, in particular, are seen as schools of last resort: overcrowded, in disrepair, lacking in basic supplies and books, and producing high dropout rates (see, e.g., Horbar, 2006). The stratification of educational opportunities in Chicago is occurring in other cities as well where the majority of schools are held to rigidly defined curricula while "successful" schools (generally in more middle-class communities) are given greater flexibility (e.g., Hoff, 2003).

Chicago is deeply etched with the social, spatial, and economic inequalities along lines of race, ethnicity, and class that define the new economy. From the Magnificent Mile, to the refurbished lakeshore, to sprawling tracts of gentrification, to the dismantling of public housing, to the racial gap in earnings, Chicago instantiates neoliberal urban development. Chicago's school reform is situated in relation to the restructured economy—a highly segmented and stratified labor force, gentrification, and displacement of working-class and low-income communities, particularly communities of color, and Chicago's drive to become a first tier "global city." Global cities are command centers of global production, financial transactions, and innovations central to the global economy (Sassen, 2006). Both high-paid professionals and low-paid service workers concentrate here. They are dual cities marked by glittering skyscrapers and downtown development, affluent gated communities and glamour zones of arts, shopping, restaurants, and recreation *and* by disinvestment in low-income working-class neighborhoods of people of color and immigrants.

In *High Stakes Education*, I contend that Chicago's school reform is a strategic element in making Chicago a global city by (a) preparing students with the basic skills and disciplined dispositions needed in the new flexible workforce, (b) developing selective schools to market the city to highly skilled knowledge workers and to increase the middle-class tax base, (c) increasing Chicago's competitive position in the world economy, and (d) disciplining and regulating students of color who are largely viewed by capital and political elites as superfluous to the labor force and "dangerous" to the global city's image. Looking at the policies district wide, I argue that the practices associated with accountability and the expansion of stratified educational options concretely and symbolically produce an economically polarized labor force and racially and socially polarized urban space. For example, the new selective magnet high schools are mostly located in gentrifying areas while scripted direct instruction schools and military academies are in low-income communities of color. These new forms of educational differentiation reproduce and expand the opportunity-to-learn gap between students who are middle class and White and students who are low-income and African American or Latino. This has grave consequences in a barbell economy in which education is more determinant than ever of who will get which jobs.

Highly differentiated educational experiences teach children to be specific kinds of people. In these schools, children are apprenticed to a specific discourse (a set of languages, practices, social relations) that construct "truths" about who they are. These identities are also projected into popular media and become part of common sense understandings. For example, military schools are known for their strict regimentation and military-style discipline that is framed as appropriate to African American and some Latino students who are by inference, undisciplined and in need of regimentation and control (Lipman, 2003). On the other hand, college preparatory magnet schools have a full menu of curricular choices, critical dialogues, and spaces of relative student freedom in a college campus ambience. The most elite among them are disproportionately White. These differentiations have important material and ideological implications for students' identities, and they help define the racial order of the city. Of course, many youth refuse to acquiesce to coercive and regimented schooling and curriculum with little meaning for them. In Chicago, as elsewhere, they simply vote with their feet—as evidenced by Chicago's high dropout rates. (Only 54% of CPS students who were 13 years old in 1998 graduated by age 19 in 2004, and only 39% of African American males graduated by age 19, Allensworth, 2005.)

Stratified education is nothing new in the United States, but because of the centrality of knowledge in the new economy, the highly polarized nature of the labor market, and the dualization of every aspect of life—from housing to health care to access to the social amenities of the city—who has access to what kind of education has perhaps greater implications than ever before. Chicago's new forms of educational differentiation put students on course for college, semiskilled vocations, the low-wage workforce, the military, or prison. This differentiation is highly racialized.

Intensifying the Equity Gap and Disciplining African American Students

During my research, I conducted case studies of the meanings of Chicago's accountability policies in four elementary schools. The case studies illustrate the racialized nature of education accountability as it is actually lived in schools. Two of the schools, Grover and Westview, served very low-income African American students living in public housing projects. In CPS terms, Grover was a "failing school" on probation and Westview an "improving school." During the time I studied them (1998–2001) the city began the process of demolishing 18,000 units of public housing and displacing residents, including students at both schools. The buildings have now been leveled and the neighborhoods are now sites of large condominium and upscale townhouse development. I want to highlight two implications for African American students as accountability policies played out at Grover and Westview.

First, I found that, despite some improvements, on balance, the practices engendered by accountability did not narrow disparities in curriculum, quality of teaching, or educational opportunities between these schools and the others I studied that were not predominantly African American. With some exceptions, rather than enrich teaching and learning and promote the sorts of literacies and academic dispositions prized in the new economy, accountability policies promoted a narrow focus on skills to pass high-stakes tests. At Grover, probation and the school's changing array of external supervisors produced incoherent and routinized approaches that did little to improve instruction and that undermined the few teachers with an orientation to rich literacies and culturally relevant teaching. Some Westview teachers tried to avoid this routinization but were required to put away the regular curriculum for 13 weeks of test prep. Accountability redefined a "good school" solely as a high-scoring school. In this discourse, Grover became a somewhat "better" school as its test scores inched up and as instruction became more systematic and standardized. Westview became quite a "good" school as its test scores approached 50% of students at or above grade level on the high-stakes test. But both schools became dominated by discourses of test preparation. At Grover, although a few incompetent teachers were pushed out, so were some of the strongest, with a vision of education that was critical, antiracist, culturally relevant, and holistic—including teachers deeply rooted in the community.

Second, the regime of inspection, testing, probation, and student retention individualized failure and instigated a circular culture of blame targeting principals, teachers, students, and parents, thereby masking the state's responsibility for the structural roots of the failure of schools like Grover to educate African American children. A Grover teacher said it was, "Like a hammer just knocking them down." Moreover, policies that regulate and punish schools in African American communities contribute to the representation of these communities, and especially Black youth, as undisciplined and in need of control. A Grover teacher said, "the administration keeps this probation climate going so strongly that I think the parents feel like they are on probation, their kids are on probation and the whole community is on probation." Colorblind policies (i.e., everyone is held to the same standards and tests) obfuscated the history of inequality and racism that has permeated the city and the school system historically. Grover and Westview were working with woefully inadequate and outdated resources—deficiencies that would never be tolerated for more affluent and White schools and communities. Until the demolition of the housing projects drastically reduced enrollment, there were more than 30 students even in primary-level classes, Grover had no functioning library or playground; neither school had functioning computers for students, and both were forced to rely on outside programs and grants to supplement their staff and programs. Ignoring these sedimented inequalities and injustices, the subtext of punitive policies was that these communities were responsible for their own "failure."

There is a record of failing to concentrate significant resources in these schools, and they were embedded in an economic system and racial order that has bred disinvestment, deindustrialization, economic impoverishment, and social crises in African American communities. Both school communities had an average annual family income of approximately $7,000 and unemployment of more than 90%. Yet, accountability policies put the onus for academic improvement on the shoulders of teachers and students and parents, feeding a cycle of blame. This dynamic resonated with, and reproduced, the neoliberal discourse of individual responsibility and blame that is lodged against those who have been the recipients of entrenched inequalities.

The Politics of Cultural Assimilation

A third school, Brewer, located in a low-income immigrant Latino community, was known as a "successful" school. In 1995, Brewer was poised for change. Multiple and competing educational philosophies and ideologies were at work, but the school had a core of committed culturally relevant teachers, a bold new Latino principal committed to the community, a humanistic educational vision, and bilingual/bicultural education. Under his leadership, the school began an extraordinary process of reflection, self-study, and dialogue that involved teachers, administrators, staff, students, and allied university faculty. The process began to openly address issues of race, culture, and power that are central to the inequalities and injustices in urban schools but largely absent from educators' public discussions (Lipsitz, 1998). This engagement contrasted sharply with intensified centralized regulation and surveillance and the incentives and punishments that characterize CPS's accountability system and NCLB. Brewer's process could be interpreted as a potential counter to those who argue that there is no alternative to top-down accountability and surveillance as the way to improve urban schools. It also speaks to how destructive these policies can be to a genuine attempt to challenge entrenched, middle-class assumptions and racist ideologies and practices in schools.

Over the years of participating in the school, co-researcher Eric Gutstein and I saw this process and seeds of liberatory education—critical approaches to knowledge, culturally relevant teaching, and support for bilingual literacies— undermined by dominant CPS policies (Lipman & Gutstein, 2004). For example, teachers abandoned a conceptual mathematics curriculum, in part, because they were afraid it wouldn't prepare students for the high-stakes standardized test. As the accountability agenda dominated more and more of the mandates emanating from the school district headquarters, and as test scores became the sole official determinant of a school's effectiveness, this agenda overcame a school-based process of critical reflection. The CPS program gave validation to the teachers who had opposed or resisted this process.

Brewer also illustrates how accountability policies that substitute standardization for equity undermine community struggles to center their culture, language, and history in the curriculum. As high-stakes standardized tests drive the curriculum, they reinscribe the historical subordination of the identities and knowledge of marginalized communities. At Brewer, teachers were under increasing pressure to transition Spanish-speaking students to English to meet the district's three-year limit before students must take the high-stakes test in English. We observed, and teachers reported, the reassertion of assimilationist practices, even by teachers deeply committed to bilingual/bicultural education. Ms. Guzman, a primary-level bilingual education teacher, immigrated to the community from Mexico when she was 14. Her own experiences in a monolingual–English school that disrespected her language and culture motivated her to become a bilingual teacher in her community. After four years of the district's high-stakes English transition policy, she said, "by the time I finish the year I feel like the Spanish seems to be decreasing and decreasing even more … because now they're going to take a test, and if they don't score what they're supposed to score, they're gonna be held back."

The effects extend beyond the school. Latinos are 26% of Chicago's population and the fastest growing demographic group. Teachers and parents in the Brewer community talk about the centrality of language for community cohesion and as a means of cultural contention for space and place in the city. Brewer is now a prime target of gentrification. Education policies that undercut the community's linguistic and cultural integrity weaken its cohesion and its ability to resist attempts by the city and developers to gentrify the community. At the same time, assimilationist policies serve the workforce demands of city businesses. A 1998 policy paper by the Commercial Club of Chicago (CCC), the organization of the city's most powerful corporate and financial leaders, specifically highlighted the need to improve the basic educational performance (as measured by standardized tests) of schools serving "Hispanics" "for the economy to prosper" (Johnson, 1998, p. 6). School accountability policies serve as a powerful preparation for a stratified and compliant workforce.

Intersections of Class and Race

The fourth school, Farley, was a "high-scoring" school in a mixed-income, mixed-race area. It had a racially and economically diverse student body but a powerful core of professional families with considerable political clout. Farley teachers, principals, and parents had a history of publicly standing up to the Board of Education, and many in the school and community with whom I spoke attributed this to the community's affluence and the political influence of powerful parents. Farley demonstrated that a school's experiences and accountability are quite different when that school is backed up by an economically and socially powerful community, and that enjoys sedimented race and class advantages.

Farley exemplified the educational advantages of race and class power. Many classes I observed at Farley developed the intellectual dispositions and confidence in one's ability to construct knowledge that prepares students for a future in the knowledge-driven economy. This was strikingly different from the routinized instruction I observed in many classes at Grover and in a substantial number of classes at Westview and even Brewer. The school's tradition of teaching for critical thought and promoting student dialogue also seemed to be a basis of resistance to the centralized regulation of teachers and curriculum that drove out some of the most thoughtful teachers at Grover, Westview, and Brewer. Nevertheless, the accountability regime was perceived as a threat to the school's professional culture.

Yet, there were significant racial disparities lurking beneath the surface of Farley's apparent success, and these disparities proved to weaken the school as a whole. African American students showed a pattern of lower academic achievement than White students, particularly those beginning in fourth grade did. African American parents raised concerns about these disparities and the disproportionate discipline actions taken against their children. In the year before I conducted my research, they had insisted that the school commission a study of these issues. Standardized test results, disaggregated by race under CPS policy, revealed these racial disparities. This is precisely the public rationale for introducing the accountability measures of NCLB, and Farley reveals the good sense in making these results public.

However, simply publishing the results did little to challenge underlying inequities. The specter of increased surveillance under the accountability regime fostered fear of any public controversy at Farley. This worked to reinforce the school's unwillingness to examine the causes of racial disparities. Instead of addressing these issues head on, teachers and administrators responded by locating deficiencies in individual African American students and families and redoubling their remediation of the students, rather than questioning institutional practices. Thus the accountability policies did nothing to address the root cause of the problems and actually reinforced whatever notions of deficiency animated the practice and conversations of some of the teachers.

In *High Stakes Education*, I argue that the factors that make schools such as Farley strong—its knowledgeable and proactive teaching staff, rich literacy practices, holistic educational goals, and independence—are unlikely to be cultivated by top-down directives, prescriptive pedagogies, and pressures to raise test scores through endless test-preparation drills. However, I also argue that to position Farley as a model is to leave unchallenged the dominant framework of what constitutes literacy and legitimate classroom knowledge and the ways in which schools such as Farley fail students of color. It also negates the strengths of some teachers in lower scoring schools—culturally relevant teaching, commitment to and connections with low-income children of color, and critical perspectives. Although Farley's students read and produced rich texts, this did not necessarily mean they developed critical literacy or that instruction was equitable. In fact, one aspect of significant disparities in academic achievement between White and African American students at Farley was the privileging of Eurocentric knowledge and middle-class cultural capital, and the failure to foster critical perspectives. Nothing in accountability policies challenged this; if anything, they reinforced it.

Conclusions

I want to highlight two conclusions. First, the accountability policies in Chicago tend to reproduce and extend inequalities. An expanded system of choice of educational "opportunities" coupled with test-driven accountability primarily in low-income schools serving students of color creates new forms of educational inequality layered over an already unequal education system. Entrenched advantages/disadvantages were compounded by accountability and centralized regulation to produce disparities in teaching and learning and intellectual and social dispositions. A stratified system of basic skills and scripted instruction, military schools, new vocational schools, "last resort" neighborhood schools, International Baccalaureates and selective college prep schools helps reproduce a stratified labor force for the restructured economy and the deeply unequal social structure that characterizes the neoliberal global economy and global cities in particular.

Second, everyday practices of high-stakes testing, centralized regulation of schools and teachers, and public designation of failure work as a system of racialized social control and disempowerment. Schools in low-income communities of color are the least in charge of their own destiny. In the schools under the most pressure to raise test scores (schools serving low-income students of color) accountability is a panoptic system of surveillance that teaches people to comply and to discipline themselves. Without real public discussion or the participation of teachers, school administrators, students, and parents, powerful city and school officials hold up these schools, and by implication, their communities, as examples of failure, determine what will happen in their schools, and undermine community-led Local School Councils (LSCs). The regimented practices associated with high-stakes accountability, scripted direct instruction, and military schools are racially coded signifiers that African American students in particular, and, by extension, their communities, need regulation and control (see Lipman, 2003). It is a form of colonial governance that signals that these communities do not have the capacity to act together with educators to improve their children's education. This takes on particular significance in a context in which racialized containment, control, and displacement are central to the neoliberal restructuring of the economy.

Chicago's Renaissance 2010

I want to elaborate this point by briefly discussing the direction the Chicago public school system has taken recently and the implications for race and class inequality. In June 2004, Mayor Daley announced Renaissance 2010 (Ren2010), a plan to further revamp CPS. The first stage is to close 60 to 70 schools (on grounds of failure and/or underutilization) and open 100 new schools, two-thirds as charter or contract schools. These schools will have neither LSCs nor will they be covered by existing school employee unions. As of spring 2006, 18 schools were approved to close, all in African American communities. This plan is an example of efforts to privatize public education nationally and of another way education is being put to the service of a larger neoliberal project (see also Cucchiara, 2006).

The outline of the Ren2010 plan was proposed by the Civic Committee of the CCC in a July 2003 report (Civic Committee). The CCC promised to raise $50 million to help fund the initiative, and it created New Schools for Chicago, a public-private partnership to coordinate its involvement. Chicago's failure to make Adequate Yearly Progress (AYP) toward NCLB benchmarks and the potential for a state takeover are major themes running through the CCC's argument for a quasi-market solution of school choice and charter schools. Disenchanted with the pace of reform, the CCC contends, "Competition—which is the engine of American productivity generally—is the key to improved performance of our public schools" (p. 55).

I have been studying Ren2010 since the plan was announced. In addition to policy documents, archival data, and following school board meetings and public hearings, I have observed and participated in the multiple forms of resistance that students, families, community members, school reform groups, and teachers have been waging against this plan, including testifying at school board meetings, public hearings, picket lines, and community organizing activities of all sorts, primarily with south side and west side African American communities. Three themes from my observations and interviews illustrate the implications of Ren2010 for equity and justice in the city.

First, Ren2010 undermines the democratic participation of communities of color in institutions integral to their lives. Elimination of participatory democracy in favor of closed-door decisions by appointed corporate bodies and experts is a key feature of neoliberalism. This closely mirrors the Ren2010 process thus far and is a major complaint of community residents who insist they have not been consulted about decisions that deeply affect them. The evidence shows that CPS and city officials have consistently excluded African American community members and devalued the knowledge and commitments of teachers in the schools affected. CPS has announced plans to close schools with just a few days or weeks notice, and some teachers and administrators learned their school was slated to be closed by reading about it in the newspaper. Frustration with the failure to invite the authentic participation of families and community members is a central theme in rallies, community forums, press conferences, school board testimony, and information disseminated to the public by those opposed to Ren2010.

Community exclusion is codified by the elimination of LSCs in Ren2010 charter and contract schools. LSCs are one of the few institutionalized forms of local democratic participation in the city. Ren2010 further weakens LSCs that were already limited by accountability policies. This has important implications for political disempowerment of communities of color in the face of a corporate agenda for the city. The CCC's New Schools for Chicago, an unelected corporate body, participates in the selection of new Ren2010 schools and evaluation of their performance. In place of community elected LSCs, a corporate body is making decisions about schools in Black communities. This reinscription of colonial governance represents the racialized character of the neoliberal impetus to suppress democracy in favor of efficiency, governance by experts, and direct corporate control (Harvey, 2005).

Second, the failure of the schools being closed and their underutilization is tied to a history of disinvestment in African American schools and communities. Parents and teachers cited the incoherence created by a revolving door of mandated initiatives for schools on probation and the lack of resources to succeed. Schools slated for closing had a history of cuts in educational support staff, a shortage of text books, and buildings needing repair in the years prior to Ren2010. In my field notes from Board of Education meetings, there is a consistent pattern of parents and teachers from schools in the African American west and south sides of the city coming to appeal for basic building repairs (a working furnace, windows that open, an elevator for physically disabled students, repairs to rotted plumbing) and for text books, additional classrooms, and basic supplies.

Third, school closings have been concentrated in African American neighborhoods experiencing gentrification. A persistent theme in community hearings in these areas is that closing schools is part of a larger plan to push residents out of the community to further gentrification. As an illustration, the first target of Ren2010 was the Midsouth, where 20 of 22 schools were slated to close until organized community opposition thwarted the plan. The Midsouth is one of the most intensely gentrifying areas in the city as reflected in rate of house sales, increase in house prices, and sheer numbers of new units being developed. Part of this development is on a several mile stretch of land where the largest complex of high-rise public housing projects in the city was located. The city housing authority has demolished most of the buildings and in their wake rise block after block of townhouses, condominiums, and single-family homes ranging from more than $200,000 to more than $500,000. As African American residents see their neighborhoods being transformed, they contend that the new schools are not designed for them. A community member and 34-year veteran teacher crystallized this sentiment: "We're being pushed out of the city under the guise of school reform."

Ren2010 and the Neoliberal Urban Agenda

Claims that gentrification is a motivating factor that can be assessed by looking at the global economic and political forces shaping the city, Neil Smith argues that gentrification, has become "a central motive force of urban economic expansion, a pivotal sector in the new urban economies" (Smith, 2002, p. 447). Gentrification as a neoliberal capital accumulation strategy is facilitated by public-private partnerships that use public funds for private development. Michaels Development Company (whose development projects in cities across the United States are funded overwhelmingly by public dollars) has a $600 million investment in Legends South, a complex of more than 2,300 houses and apartments on a two mile stretch of land where the Robert Taylor Homes public housing complex stood. The entire city landscapes are transformed into gentrification "complexes" of consumption, recreation, culture, parks, and schools as well as housing by twenty-first century gentrification. It is in this context that we can interpret the strategic importance of closing schools. Closing schools contribute to pushing families out of the neighborhoods. The schools are then revamped and reopened later as new schools, with new identities, offering a range of choices to new middle-class residents. For example, CPS created a public Montessori school on the west side of the city in place of a neighborhood school that formerly serviced public housing residents. The new school has almost entirely middle-class enrollment.

Smith (2002) argues that although gentrification is cast as a positive strategy to "regenerate" decaying urban areas, it is actually a strategy to regenerate profits and a means for the middle- and upper middle class to colonize the city. For example, of approximately 27,000 displaced residents in Robert Taylor Homes public housing project, more than 22,000 will not have housing in Legends South, the new mixed income development replacing Robert Taylor. Sudhir Venkatesh, a Columbia University sociologist who is tracking the relocation of public housing residents, estimates conservatively that less than 20% of residents will be able to return to their old neighborhood (Venkatesh, Celimli, Miller, Murphy, & Turner, 2004). The class nature of gentrification is obscured by the language of the "frontier" and rebirth, a language rooted in the demonization of low-income people of color to be displaced (Smith). Before communities can become new sites of capital accumulation, they have to be devalued, prepared for development, and reimagined as places of value. The discourse of blame surrounding the "failure" of low-income African American and Latino schools contributes to the devaluation of the communities. Closing these schools and later opening new schools with new identities (sometimes in the same buildings) is part of a cultural politics of race that is central to appropriating the resources of communities of color, privatizing them, and displacing the residents. This trend increasingly characterizes the neoliberal restructuring of the city and is a principle factor in the growing inequality in metropolitan regions.

Literacy as a Civil Right

In the present economic and political context, literacy, and what kinds of literacies students master, is a critical issue for economic survival and political participation. Gee, Hull, and Lankshear (1996) point out,

> The new capitalism is in danger of producing and reproducing an even steeper pyramid than the old capitalism did. And, just as in the old capitalism, it will need institutions—like schools, first and foremost—to reproduce that social structure. (p. 47)

Acquisition of the knowledge, skills, and forms of literacy that are highly valued in the new economy is critical if students are to have access to higher education and job opportunities that offer a degree of economic security and well-being. In a barbell economy and a society that offers little in the way of social welfare, full access to literacy is a civil right. Its denial is part of relegating whole communities to the low-wage, military, and prison-prep tracks in society.

Beyond equal access, students need critical literacies to survive and challenge the deep inequalities and structures of power we face. Critically reading the media, popular culture, and texts in order to better read the world is a crucial aspect of critical consciousness and collective action. This is concrete and immediate in the present historical moment of profound inequality, preemptive war as foreign policy, and potential ecological disaster. Yet these literacies are further undermined by instruction driven by high-stakes tests and mandated scripts and by militarized schooling for children of color. A society producing growing contrasts of wealth and poverty, centrality and marginality, requires both the domestication of critical thought and agency and coercion to maintain social control. The cultural politics of race and the social control of communities of color, particularly youth, are central to these goals. We cannot fully understand the implications of education policies outside this context.

What counts as literacy for which students is highly contested, and the stakes are high. This implies much about the important roles and responsibilities of educators to work within existing constraints to put social justice at the center of literacy work in schools. It also suggests, as Jean Anyon (2005) notes, that educators cannot confine their participation to the classroom if they hope to do this work. It will require social movements of communities, students, and educators to challenge the neoliberal education agenda and the larger neoliberal economic and social agenda and to pose alternatives grounded in social justice. There are rumblings of these movements in local campaigns against high-stakes tests, student walkouts for immigrant rights, resistance to Ren2010 in Chicago, and the youth organizations and critical cultural productions of youth outside the school walls. The future leaders of social movements are in our classrooms, especially in urban schools of color where the race, class, and gender contradictions of neoliberal economic and social policy are most sharp. Perhaps supporting their critical consciousness and agency is the standard against which to judge the literacy work of k-12 and university teachers in dangerous times.

Notes

1. The New York Times reported that 35% of the city's Black residents—almost 110,000 people—were living in poverty, according to the 2000 census.
2. Harvey (2005) reports that the net worth of the 358 richest people in 1996 equaled the combined income of the poorest 45% of the world's population—2/3 billion people and the world's 200 richest people more than doubled their wealth to more than $1 trillion from 1994 to 1998 (pp. 34–35).
3. The ARC cites data from the Center for Tax and Budget Accountability that show that Blacks are 15 percent of the metropolitan Chicago workforce but 30 percent of the working poor, and Latinos are 10 percent of the workforce but 27 percent of the working poor (ARC, 2007, p.14).
4. After World War II, capital traded increased wages and benefits for workers for labor stability and acceptance of U.S. imperial policies abroad. This compact plus Keynesian welfare state policies raised the standard of living and social security of White workers in particular (see Barlow, 2003; Lipsitz, 1998).

References

Allensworth, E. (2005). Graduation and dropout trends in Chicago: A look at cohorts of students from 1991 through 2004. Chicago: Consortium on Chicago School Research.

Anyon, J. (2005). *Radical possibilities*. New York: Routledge.

Apple, M. W. (2001). *Educating the "right" Way*. New York: Routledge.

Applied Research Center. (2006). *Illinois Legislative Report Card on Racial Equity*. Chicago: Author.

Aronowitz, S., & Giroux, H. A. (1993). *Education still under siege*, 2nd ed. Westport, CT: Bergin & Garvey.

Ball, S. J. (1994). *Education Reform: A Critical and Post-structural Approach*, Buckingham, England: Open University Press.

Barlow, A. L. (2003). *Between fear and hope: Globalization and race in the United States*. Lanham, MD: Rowman & Littlefield.

Bonilla-Silva, E. (2003). *Racism without racists*. Lanham, MD: Rowman & Littlefield.

Brown, E. (2003). Freedom for Some, Discipline for "Others." In K. L. Saltman & D. Gabbard (Eds.) *Education as Enforcement* (pp. 127–151). New York: Routledge.

Castells, M. (1989). *The informational city*. London: Blackwell.

Center for Tax & Budget Accountability and Northeastern Illinois University. (2005.) *The State of Working Illinois*. Chicago & DeKalb, IL: Author.

Civic Committee of the Commercial Club of Chicago. (2003, July). Left behind. A report of the Education Committee. Chicago: Author. Retrieved July 30, 2006 from http://www.commercialclubchicago.org/civiccommittee/initiatives/education/student-achievement.htm

Cucchiara, M. (2006). A "Higher Class" of School Reform: Downtown Schools, Middle-Class Parents, and Urban Revitalization. Paper presented at the Annual Meeting of the Urban Affairs Association. Montreal, MD.

Dale, R. (1989/1990). The Thatcherite project in education: The case of the City Technology Colleges. *Critical Social Policy, 9*(3), 4–19.

Duggan, L. (2003). *The Twilight of Inequality? Neoliberalism, cultural politics and the attach on democracy*. Boston: Beacon Press.

Gee, J. P., Hull, G., & Lankshear, C. (1996). The new work order: Behind the language of the new capitalism. Boulder, CO: Westview Press.

Gill, S. (2003). *Power and resistance in the new world order*. New York: Palgrave Macmillan.

Haney, W. (2000). The myth of the Texas miracle in education. *Educational Policy Archives, 8*(41). Retrieved August 30, 2000, from http://epaa.asu.edu/epaa/v8n41

Haney, W. (2001). Revisiting the myth of the Texas miracle in education: Lessons about dropout research and dropout prevention. Paper prepared for the "Dropout Research: Accurate Counts and Positive Interventions" Conference Sponsored by Achieve and the Harvard Civil Rights Project. Cambridge, MA.

Haney, W. (2003). Attrition of students from New York schools. Invited testimony before New York Senate Standing Committee on Education. Retrieved December 10, 2005, from http://www.timeoutfromtesting.org/testimonies/923_Testimony_Haney.pdf

Harvey, D. (2004). *The new imperialism*. Oxford: Oxford University Press.

Harvey, D. (2005). *A brief history of neoliberalism*. Oxford: Oxford University Press.

Hoff, D. J. (2003, March 9). Complaints pour in over NYC curriculum exemptions. *Education Week*. Retrieved March 14, 2003, from http://www.edweek.org

Horbar, E. (2006, March). *Q&A with Soktheary Nak*. Catalyst: Chicago. Retrieved August 12, 2006, from http://www.catalyst-chicago.org/news/index.php?item=1944&cat=22

Hursh, D. (2004). Undermining democratic education in the USA: The consequences of global capitalism and neo-liberal policies for education policies at the local, state, and federal levels. *Policy Futures in Education, 2*(3–4), 601–614.

Hursh, D. (2005). The growth of high stakes testing in the USA: Accountability, markets, and the decline of educational equality. *British Journal of Education, 31*(5), 605–618.

Johnson, E. (1998, November). *Chicago metropolis 2020: Preparing metropolitan Chicago for the 21st century: Executive Summary.* Chicago: Commercial Club of Chicago.

Lauder, H., Brown, P., Dillabough, J., & Halsey, A. H. (2006). *Education, globalization, and social change.* Oxford: Oxford University Press.

Lipman, P. (2002). Making the global city, making inequality: The political economy and cultural politics of Chicago school policy. *American Educational Research Journal, 39*(2), 379–419.

Lipman, P. (2003). Chicago school policy: Regulating black and Latino youth in the global city. *Race, Ethnicity and Education, 6*(4), 331–355.

Lipman, P. (2004). *High stakes education: Inequality, globalization, and urban school reform.* New York: Routledge.

Lipman, P., & Gutstein, R. (2004). The policies and politics of cultural assimilation. In P. Lipman (Ed.), *High stakes education: Inequality, globalization, and urban school reform* (chap. 5). New York: Routledge.

Lipman, P., & Hursh, D. (2007). Renaissance 2010: The reassertion of ruling-class power through neoliberal policies in Chicago. *Policy Futures in Education, 5*(2). Retrieved http://www.wwwords.co.uk/pfie/content/pdfs/5/issue5_2.asp#5

Lipsitz, G. (1998). *Possessive investment in whiteness: How white people profit from identity politics.* Philadelphia: Temple University Press.

McNeil, L. M. (2000). *Contradictions of school reform: Educational costs of standardized testing.* New York: Routledge.

National Priorities Project. (1998). *Working hard, earning less: The story of job growth in Illinois.* Grassroots Factbook, Vol. I, Series 2. Author.

National Priorities Project. (2005). *Quick Report: Poverty in Illinois.* Retrieved September 11, 2006, from http://database.nationalpriorities.org/cgi-bin/WebObjects/nppdatabase.woa/1/wo/lxedaDz7fdFah91h0Q1xag/23.0.1.1.6

Neil, M., Guisbond, L., & Schaeffer, B. (2004). *Failing our children: How "No Child Left Behind" undermines quality and equity in education.* Cambridge, MA: Fair Test, National Center for Fair and Open Testing.

No Child Left Behind. U.S. Department of Education. Retrieved February 10, 2002, from http://www.ed.gov/inits/nclb

Parenti, C. (1999). *Lockdown America: Police and prisons in the age of crisis.* London: Verso.

Poverty Summit. (2006). *2006 Report on Illinois Poverty.* Chicago: Heartland Alliance. Retrieved September 30, 2006, from http://www.heartlandalliance.org

Saltman, K. (2005). *The Edison schools: Corporate schools and the assault on public education.* New York: Routledge Falmer.

Sassen, S. (2006). *Cities in a world economy (3rd ed).* Thousand Oaks, CA: Pine Forge Press.

Skinner, C. (2004). The changing occupational structure of large metropolitan areas: Implications for the high school educated. *Journal of Urban Affairs, 26*(1), 67–88.

Smith, N. (1996). *The new urban frontier: Gentrification and the revanchist city.* New York: Routledge.

Smith, N. (2002). New globalism, new urbanism: Gentrification as global urban strategy. *Antipode, 34*(3), 427–450.

Tomlinson, S. (2005). *Education in a post-welfare society (2nd ed)*. Maidenhead, UK: Open University Press.

Valenzuela, A. (Ed.). (2005). *Leaving children behind: How "Texas-style" accountability fails Latino youth*. Albany: State University of New York Press.

Venkatesh, S. A., Celimli, I., Miller, D., Murphy, A., & Turner, B. (2004, February). Chicago Public Housing transformation: A research report. New York: Center for Urban Research and Policy, Columbia University.

Wacquant, L. (2001). The penalization of poverty and the rise of neoliberalism. *European Journal of Criminal Policy and Research, 9*(4), 401–412.

Whitty, G., Power, S., & Halpin, D. (1999). *Devolution and choice in education: The school, the state, and the market*. Buckingham, England: Open University Press.

Williams, D. (2006, February). Great expectations for King Prep come up short. *Catalyst: chicago*. Retrieved August 29, 2006, from http://www.catalyst-chicago.org/news/index.php?item=1912&cat=23

II

HOW RACE IS LIVED
IN SCHOOLS

· 3 ·

"EVEN SWEET, GENTLE LARRY?"
THE CONTINUING SIGNIFICANCE
OF RACE IN EDUCATION

AMANDA E. LEWIS

In 1979 William Julius Wilson published a book titled, *The Declining Significance of Race* and in it, the first line is as follows: "Race relations in America have undergone fundamental changes in recent years, so much so that now the life chances of individual blacks have more to do with their economic class position than with their day-to-day encounters with whites" (p. 1) He argued that while in the past

> Blacks were denied access to valued and scarce resources through various ingenious schemes of racial exploitation, discrimination, and segregation, schemes that were reinforced by elaborate ideologies of racism ... the situation has changed ... they do not provide a meaningful explanation of the life changes of black Americans today. (p. 1)

A vast body of sociological work followed, including some by Wilson himself, demonstrating that the significance of race in shaping life opportunities had not disappeared.

In this chapter, I am concerned with the significance of race in school achievement. I want to focus both on how we think about race inside and outside of schools and on how race shapes school experiences including the role of our wider, racialized social context in shaping school outcomes. I began thinking about this work almost 10 years ago while I was in my second or third student-teaching placement in California. One day at the beginning of this placement,

I sat in the lunchroom with a teacher and principal while they talked about the disciplinary referrals they had doled out thus far that year. I was working in a third-grade classroom, part of a respected metropolitan school district. The teacher was a charismatic, energetic middle-aged White woman, the principal an efficient and authoritative African American woman. The school population, as well as that of my classroom, was about half White and half African American. As is not unusual in this kind of deliberately desegregated space, it was also true that the White children were from primarily middle- and upper-middle-class homes, while the Black children came from primarily working-class or poor homes. In our classroom were six African American boys, each of different appearance, temperament, family background, achievement level, and disposition. Kendrick was tall, athletic, extroverted, and bright. Larry was short, bookish, amiable, and round. Antoine was boisterous, fidgety, and charming, part of a program to mainstream children with special educational designations (in his case a severe emotional impairment). The others were equally different.

As a new and nervous teacher, I wanted to know which children in the class had had disciplinary problems so far in the year. My cooperating teacher and the principal began to name the children who had received referrals thus far. It was when they got to Larry that I sat dumbfounded, realizing that they had named every single Black male from our class. As I casually asked if that was all, they declared proudly that that had been it (it was a relatively small total for the year), unaware that they had named all and *only* African American males. "Even sweet, gentle Larry?" I thought. Larry, who regularly spent his recess reading a book on the shadiest bench in the yard and answered every question posed to him with a broad and eager smile?

I left that interaction wanting to know how such a pattern could occur and even more, how responsible adults with the best intentions could describe it without noticing, without expressing alarm. I knew all of us wanted schools to serve every student well, and yet there were major racial differentials in school outcomes. What was going on, I wondered. How was race shaping experiences and outcomes in schools? What role did it play in our everyday interactions there? As a young teacher, I had been given no tools to understand how race was going to affect what happened in the classroom—how it might shape what happened between teacher and student, between students, and between school personnel and parents. I did not have ready access to the language with which to describe, much less to challenge what I began to see every day. In schools, we cannot begin to change these kinds of racial dynamics without first being able to describe them and talk about them.

In this chapter, I begin by focusing on just what race is and why it matters. I briefly define race, outline how it shapes our social locations, and focus on how it works in our everyday lives in schools. One of our largest and deepest problems in both scholarly and commonsense discussions of race in education is how often we operate with oversimplified or inaccurate conceptualizations of just what race is. In some ways, our inaccurate notions mean we attribute significance to race that it does not have and in other cases our misconceptions mean we underestimate its effects. In either case, I argue that we cannot advance an agenda of reclaiming social justice in education generally much less in literacy research and teaching without a frank, honest, and informed discussion about persisting relevance of race.

What is Race?

Race is not something we are born with. Rather, it is something that is mapped onto us from the first moments of life (with the listing of race on our birth certificate). We must *learn* how to categorize ourselves and others, what the available options are, the boundaries between categories, and what it means to belong to one grouping rather than another. Because we tend to treat racial categories as fixed, they appear to be natural or permanent. However, these classifications are not natural or biological facts that exist beyond specific historical contexts.

Race is best understood as a salient social category. Biologists and anthropologists have long agreed that the idea of "pure" races is a genetic absurdity since most genetic inheritance is shared in common by all the major populations groups. Clearly there are phenotypic differences between us. But those superficial differences we use to define each other "racially" do not translate into widespread biological differences between populations groups (American Anthropological Association, 1998; Begley, 1995; Graves, 2001; Lieber, 1994).[1] We all originally come from the same place. It is true that people evolved differently depending on where they wandered off to, but the percentage of our genes that are reflected in our external appearance—the basis by which we talk about race—is in the range of about .01% (Angier, 2000). There is far more diversity within what we think of as racial categories than there is between them.

Another way of thinking about the "social" rather than biological origins of racial categories is to trace their history across space and time. Racial categories and boundaries vary from society to society (e.g., a person from South Asia could simultaneously be categorized as "Black" in the United Kingdom,

Asian American in the United States, and "colored" in South Africa). Racial categories have also varied from region to region within a particular society. At the same historical moment in U.S. history, laws banning intermarriage in the United States defined "Black" varied from state to state. In Kentucky you were considered Black if you had one-quarter Black "blood," while you were Black in Indiana if you were one-eighth Black, and in Georgia and Alabama only a trace was necessary to be legally Black (Davis, 1991; Haney-Lopez, 1996). Thus, a person could walk across state lines and shift from one category to another. Similarly, Irish and Italians in the United States, now firmly ensconced within the category "White," were previously viewed as distinct races (Guglielmo, 2003; Jacobson, 1998; Roediger, 1991). Even today, groups are attempting to be racially reclassified: Hawaiians successfully petitioned to be categorized as Native American rather than "Asian Pacific Islander" for the 2000 census, and Arab Americans petitioned not to be classified as "White." Although we continue to think we "see" race when we look at others, we are instead seeing superficial differences that persist in their significance because of the meaning we attribute to them.

However, racial categories are not merely sociological abstractions. They are potent social groupings around which people organize their identities and behavior and that influence their opportunities and outcomes. In this way, though not natural qualities, racial classifications are socially "real." As American sociologist W. I. Thomas said, "When people define situations as real, they are real in their consequences." Across the history of the United States, placement in particular racial categories has had persistent consequences for people's lives and resulted in objective, measurable differences in life circumstances.

In a society such as ours, where racial meaning and categories are relevant and enforced, and where racial differences are naturalized, race shapes self-understanding, interaction with others, institutional practices, and access to material resources. In fact, in recent years there has been much debate in the popular and social science literature about whether race or class is more important for shaping life opportunities. In many ways, it is a debate that falsely assumes you can talk about one without talking about the other. We can see this fallacy when we examine issues of wealth. In the United States, we tend to think of social class as something captured by family income or how much money you bring in at the end of the month. Moreover, while income clearly matters for quality of life, it is in many ways less important than another key socioeconomic variable that we often ignore—wealth. We ignore wealth not because we think it doesn't matter but because information about it is hard to come by. You can guess someone's income based on their profession, but you cannot guess how much money they inherited from their grandparents or whether their parents gave them the down payment for their home. Net wealth includes all one's material resources (home, car, stocks, bonds, and savings) minus their debt. In 1994, the median net worth for White families in the United States was approximately $57,000. The median net worth for African American families was approximately $1,000 (Oliver & Shapiro, 1995; Wolff, 2001). Even middle-class Black families have less wealth than working-class White families. A majority of wealth accumulation is driven by intergenerational transfers, and racial differences in wealth are the cumulative effect of centuries of racial discrimination (Wolff, 2001). There is no doubt that our socioeconomic status matters for our life outcome, but we cannot understand aggregate group-level patterns in resource acquisition without paying attention to race and history. There is ample and clear evidence of those historic wealth acquisition opportunities available to Whites and systematically denied to Blacks (Katznelson, 2005; Lipsitz, 1998). These factors are in addition to and go far beyond just the wages denied during hundreds of years of slavery and the enforced subordination of a hundred years of Jim Crow segregation. Just one example of the kinds of public policies and private practices that lead to such dramatic wealth differentials comes out of the creation of the Federal Housing Administration (FHA), which made home ownership possible for millions of Americans who would otherwise never have been able to afford it. By backing mortgages made at low interest rates over long periods, the FHA supported a rapid transformation in home ownership patterns in the United States. It is well documented that a key part of FHA policy included explicit institutionalized racism in the form of the federal underwriting manual and guidelines (Katznelson, 2005; Massey & Denton, 1993). These guidelines declared neighborhoods with even one or two non-Whites as "high risk" and redlined most Black communities in cities throughout the country. Between 1934 and 1962, the federal government underwrote more than $100 billion in new housing. Less than 2% went to Blacks (Lipsitz, 1998).

The income gap between Black and White families persists—White families on average earn much more. But this gap is minor in scale and consequence when compared to gaps in wealth. As sociologist Thomas Shapiro put it, "Wealth represents the sedimentation of historical inequalities in the American experience, in a sense the accumulation of advantages and disadvantages for different racial, class, and ethnic groups" (Shapiro, 2005, p. 65) Moreover, recent research convincingly demonstrates the educational payoffs wealth has for White families who can draw on such family resources in selecting the best neighborhoods and schools (Johnson, 2006; Shapiro, 2004). Johnson (2006) and Johnson and Shapiro (2003) show that race has the multiple effects of providing Whites with resources to ensure their children get the best education available and also shapes Whites' decisions about where to send their children to school. Like Saporito and Lareau (1999), they find that Whites use race as a proxy for school quality, avoiding majority minority schools.

Whereas we often do not understand the many ways that race shapes our life experiences and educational outcomes, we sometimes assume race matters in ways it does not. For example, gaps in school outcomes are often explained as a result of racial differences in values, the result of minority peers discouraging each other from achieving, or because of deficient family practices. But, recent research by sociologist Dalton Conley shows that when you control for wealth, racial differences in a whole range of social outcomes such as high school graduation and college completion disappear entirely (Conley, 1999). Moreover, research on family life and school outcomes shows that Black middle-class families work just as hard to ensure their children succeed as do their White middle-class counterparts (Lareau, 2003). That is, they enroll them in multiple educational and athletic activities, work hard to get them into good schools, set high expectations for them. However, unlike the White middle-class families, the Black parents must also pay attention to when and how their children will face discrimination, when and how their children's potential will be underestimated, when and where they will confront prejudicial attitudes and behaviors. The Black parents also must strategize about how to talk to their children about those times in their lives when others will carry low expectations for them or otherwise treat them poorly because of their race.

One of the most popular theories about why Black students underperform in school is that their peers discourage them from achieving because school is seen as a "White" thing. Known as the "acting White" hypothesis (Fordham & Ogbu, 1986), this idea has taken on a life of its own in popular culture as arguably *the* explanation for Black-White achievement gaps (O'Connor, Horvat, & Lewis, 2006). Despite its popularity, a host of recent research has challenged the idea that Black students either possess an oppositional orientation toward education or reject school as a "White thing" (Ainsworth-Darnell & Downey, 1998; Carter, 2005; Horvat & O'Connor, 2006; O'Connor, 1997, 1999; Tyson, 2002; Tyson, Darity, & Castellino, 2005).

In all questions of race, we remain collectively too focused on people's individual dispositions and ignore how racial inequality is built into our larger structures and organizations. Race affects where we live, who we interact with, and how we understand ourselves and others. As historian Thomas Holt (1995) points out, "Race yet lives because it is part and parcel of the *means* of living" (p. 12). What I have learned in my ethnographic research in schools is that we make a mistake to overlook the significance of race in these everyday dynamics—not only because we can misinterpret the patterns of outcomes, but also because we miss opportunities to intervene.

Studying Race in an Era of Color Blindness

One of the biggest problems today in any effort to build diverse educational institutions in which all members can thrive is the trend toward "color blindness" in our collective racial common sense. This new common sense draws on the progressive rhetoric of the civil rights moment, which says that we should all be judged by the content of our characters rather than the color of our skin, and it declares this aspiration a reality. Captured in statements such as, "I am colorblind," "I don't see race," "Red, purple, yellow, pink, blue, it's all the same to me," this way of talking about race sets up a number of problems. The primary problem is that such claims are patently untrue. Recent studies reveal the persistence of color-consciousness in our thinking and behavior in a wide range of social, political, cultural, and economic arenas (Bobo, Kluegel, & Smith, 1997; Bonilla-Silva, 2003; Feagin, 2001; Forman, 2004; Forman & Lewis, 2006; Gallagher, 2003; Lewis, 2003). A useful example of this phenomenon surfaced in my research in a suburban school community (Lewis, 2001). A number of parents whom I interviewed in their homogenous suburban communities would, within the same interview, claim to be color-blind, explain that race did not matter to them and that they taught their children to treat everyone the same, and then express explicit disapproval about their child ever marrying someone of another race.

Claims of color blindness are not only false, they also mask the realities of racial inequality and make it very difficult to talk about or address them. In many organizations, this lack of recognition can lead to persistent silence on race; key organizational members may find themselves hesitant to talk about race or the racial patterns present in the institution. I once attended a presentation by seventh and eighth graders about a play they had written about racial conflict in their school. When I asked the students what teachers thought about the racial conflict they were writing about, they said that their teachers were afraid to talk about it.

As scholar Kimberlé Crenshaw (1997) has pointed out, "colorblind discourse often involves a strategy of 'noticing but not considering race,' in which, when trying to defend the fairness of a decision, one claims not even to have noticed that the [client, customer, job candidate, defendant, student] involved was black" (p. 101). This kind of statement reveals that the speaker not only noticed that the person was Black; they also recognized at some level that taking note of it had consequences for the outcome of the interaction.

For many of us, lacking the language to talk about our confusions concerning race and its meaning in our lives, any discussion of race becomes dangerous territory—we worry about making a mistake, saying the wrong thing, being "misinterpreted" as racist. Schools clearly have a unique and special role as institutions of learning. Children (and adults) bring to school multiple and complex racial understandings about their own group and others, but those understandings get negotiated every day in our educational institutions. Importantly, we too often forget that race is not a fixed and permanent feature of us individually or collectively or that ideas about race are not something we are born into but something we must learn. We assume that children come to school, arrive in their classrooms, as "Black" or as "White" or as "Latino" students, and ignore the ways these identities get assigned to them in school. We fail to pay attention to how both children's and adults' understandings about race are shaped by school. Though they clearly do not "teach" racial identity in the way they teach multiplication or punctuation, schools are settings where people acquire some version "of the rules of racial classification" and of their own racial identity (Omi & Winant, 1994, p. 60). Children learn what race means for themselves and others in the context of everyday interaction.

One example from an urban elementary school illustrates this point. One day, while standing in the park helping to supervise three classes that were out enjoying a beautiful spring day, I noticed a row of six African American boys of different ages, sizes, and hues sitting, lined up, in trouble, along a bench watching as their peers played in the park. When I asked a White third grade teacher standing with me how she thought other students interpreted discipline patterns captured at that moment by the benching, she said, "I think other kids probably do think Black boys are more unruly, but I don't think they have like any deep thoughts on why. They probably just know it as a fact."

As this teacher stated, children probably did not have any deep theories. That was precisely what was so powerful, though, that they just know "as a fact" that Black boys are unruly. As another teacher at the school put it, "[it sends the message to the other kids that] there is something wrong with them. You know, that they don't belong here. Yeah, that they really don't belong here."

In fact, all racial categories have implicit commonsense understandings that somehow "inform us" about what it means that a particular person is "White," "Black," "Latino," or "Asian." These are commonsense understandings that are so widely held that they are generally understood to be facts rather than beliefs. We know clearly from research like Claude Steele's (1999) on stereotype threat that these stereotypes penetrate deeply and affect student performance on at least standardized tests in not more broadly. To quote him, "stereotype threat" involves the "threat of being viewed through the lens of a negative stereotype, or the fear of doing something [e.g. performing badly on a standardized test] that would inadvertently confirm that stereotype" (p. 46). Multiple experimental situations confirmed that when stereotype threat arose, testers performed worse than would be predicted based on their ability. The effect for standardized tests is both to dampen Black students' performance and to lift White student performance.

Race then is something we negotiate every day inside schools. It is a part of what is happening in our many daily interpersonal interactions. It is one lens through which people read the world around them and make decisions on how to act, react, and interact. Schools do not merely inherit "Black," "White," "Asian," or "Latino" students and do not merely have to struggle with racial divisions and inequities created externally, but schools in fact participate in contesting or reproducing such divisions and inequalities and participate in the creation of racial identities and understandings.

As stated above, despite the fact that race is a part of everyday life in schools the dominant racial discourse in many schools today is one that denies the reality of race. This kind of colorblind ideology takes many forms, from teachers warning me about fourth grade girls "playing the race card" to long lectures by teachers that when we are cut, we all bleed red. It might very well be true that the *ideal* of color blindness—of living in a world where we are judged, as Martin Luther King said, not by the color of our skin but by the content of our characters—is one that is still worth holding onto as a *future* aspiration. However, today it is most often just declared it as reality. "We don't see race here. I'm colorblind. All the kids are the same to me." This denies not only the way race shapes who ends up in which school buildings, the long-term legacy it continues to have on family resources, and the way it shapes school practices and interactions. It, in fact, makes us blind to the effects of color (Fish, 1993).

My work as well as abundant work in cognitive psychology tell us to expect race to matter in our own cognitive processing of others—whether consciously or unconsciously, even if we are functioning with the best intentions. Research like Steele's (1999) work on stereotype threat tells us that race already does matter for student performance in multiple complicated ways. Denial of the persisting salience of race and/or silence about it does nothing to help us recognize or change patterns in racialized school outcomes and even less to help us understand the kinds of racial understandings students have.

Who Has Race, Anyway?

One persistent pattern in research shows that people consistently tend to talk about race as if it applies only to people of color. For example, in my own studies, I asked a parent how race had shaped her life. She replied, "I haven't been around it too much." What she meant, she clarified, was that she had not been around Black people much in her life. For her, that's what "race" meant. In fact, race shapes all of our lives in lots of different complicated ways. It is something we try to identify about people when we first meet them. It is part of the way we make sense of the social world—sorting people into known categories. But White people in the United States continue to view themselves as racially neutral or normal. Thus race most often seems relevant only when Black or Brown bodies are involved. When I explained my intended research to principals at predominantly White suburban schools, a common response was that their school was not an optimal place to study race because it was not very diverse. As they understood it, race was not happening if only White people were in the room. However, race shapes all of our lives—even and especially Whites' (Katznelson, 2005; Lewis, 2004; Lipsitz, 1998; Shapiro, 2004). If we enter a school board meeting, an executive dining room, or a faculty lounge and find only White people, that turnout is not idiosyncratic or accidental. It is assuredly related to long histories of racial exclusion, even if those discriminatory policies are not actively pursued today. Past racial discrimination in the labor market, for example, influences what kinds of "work experience" people can draw upon today in applying for promotions and better jobs, and thus who occupies the executive dining room, who serves on the board of directors, and who attends partners' meetings. Though few all-White settings continue to be the result of explicitly restrictive polices (such as restrictive covenants on housing deeds or social clubs that don't accept Blacks), many result from

less-blatant but widespread policies and practices. For example, housing segregation determines who belongs to neighborhood associations, who attends
local PTA meetings, who frequents local parks, and who shops at local stores.
These are not accidentally White spaces.

Race continues to matter for Whites in the daily advantages it provides.
Audit studies of housing, lending, and employment patterns in cities across
the country reveal ongoing high levels of discrimination (Ayres & Siegelman,
1995; Bertrand & Mullainathan, 2004; Pager & Quillian, 2005; Schuman,
Singer, Donovan, & Sellitz, 1983; Turner, Fix, & Struyk, 1991; Yinger, 1995).
In these studies, conducted by a range of nonprofit and research organizations,
equally qualified Black and White or Latino and White applicants (testers)
applied for the same job, apartment, or loan. The Blacks and Latinos with the
same profiles as their White peers were offered higher loan rates, fewer housing options, and fewer and less-desirable job opportunities than Whites. But
the findings are not merely about discrimination against Blacks and Latinos.
White testers were regularly provided *more* housing options, *more and better* job
opportunities, and *better* loan rates. Any time our explanations for patterns of
social inequality focus solely on the "losers," ignoring those who benefit, we
are well advised to be deeply suspicious (Payne, 1984).

Thinking about Race Organizationally

As housing-segregation in this country remains widespread (Massey & Denton,
1993), it is often in our schools and workplaces where we have the most (if not
the only) real, sustained contact with people of other racial groups (Jackman,
1994). These settings provide the opportunity to build positive and meaningful relationships. However, they can also function as places where stereotypes
and other folk theories of race can temper interactions and further hostility.
In *The Nature of Prejudice* (1958), Gordon Allport proposed the "contact
hypothesis," asserting that under certain conditions, contact with members of
another racial group improves attitudes between the groups. The improvement
requires that four conditions be met: the groups must be of equal status, have
common goals, not be in competition, and have their contact sanctioned by
those in authority.

In many organizations, some if not all of these conditions are violated.
Rather than considering how to make good use of diversity, we often
assume that we have succeeded just by getting people into the same building,

classroom, or office. For example, one important question to ask in any school building or other organizational context to clarify the real state of affairs with regard to status, is how power is distributed in the organization. Demographic diversity within any organization does not automatically yield a multicultural community in which all stakeholders have a voice. In schools, particularly in urban schools, those who are in the numeric majority (often Black and Brown children and families) frequently have the least power. This disequilibrium can exist even in schools that are consciously trying to shift the balance of power. The disparity often becomes evident during times of conflict. At one of the schools where I was doing research, the conflict erupted around a discussion of whether or not to have school uniforms. The mostly working-class Latino parents, whose children represented two-thirds of the students, proposed and strongly supported the idea. The school's other main constituency, mostly middle-class White parents, disagreed, claiming that uniforms did not allow their children to express themselves creatively. The eventual solution was a "compromise," in which Fridays were "school spirit days" and kids were encouraged to wear school t-shirts. This conciliatory gesture constituted the extent of the school's response to the pro-uniform parents. In this and other struggles, the school's general attempt to be democratic and facilitate the success of all students fell apart whenever conflict erupted. Though teachers in the school recognized the problems with the outcome of the uniform conflict, they were under tremendous pressure from the district to retain White middle-class families in the public schools and thus, to keep them happy. When a group exerts its power and influence to gain its own ends to the detriment of a less-powerful group, possibilities of building strong and positive relationships obviously diminish. In this way, racial inequality gets reproduced through organizational dynamics.

This type of dynamics can dominate even seemingly humdrum issues, even such prosaic matters as where events are held. For example, in the segregated neighborhoods of most major U.S. cities today, organizational events like holiday parties may repeatedly take place in locations that are inconvenient if not inhospitable for some members of the organization. For example, in an urban school located in a predominantly White area of the city most of the Black and Latino students were bused in from far-flung neighborhoods. When their parents did not turn out in high numbers to evening school events it was read by faculty as lack of interest or support in education rather than as resulting from lack of transportation or child care. The school building in this way was not, as the almost all White faculty understood it, a neutral location.

After conversation between the principal and the school secretary, there was a move to hold some events in community centers nearer to many of the families' homes. This not only changed the demographics at such events but also communicated to parents that the school valued their participation and recognized the barriers they faced.

Another key related issue is how and where diversity is represented in the organization—who holds administrative and managerial positions and thus decision-making power? Even when schools have diversity on their staff, White personnel are often overrepresented in positions of power and prestige, while people of color are overrepresented in the lower-status support staff. This pattern mirrors general racial hierarchies and has multiple consequences for people of color. Not only does it affect whether personnel are aware of subtle exclusionary dynamics as those described above, but also can be of consequence for employment patterns. When decision-making power on hiring and promotion is concentrated within the hands primarily of White managers and employers, racial difference can exert a subtle but important influence. Not only cultural conflicts but also segregated social networks give the edge to those who are racially similar, particularly with regard to high-status positions.

Moreover, for the few people of color who occupy nonsupport positions, the burdens on them can be significant. These burdens can range from being asked to do much more formal service work within organizations that, for instance need diversity represented on committees, to having to do the extra social and psychological work of regularly putting people at ease with their presence. For example, at many schools that have few teachers of color on staff, those minority faculty members are too often expected to be the "go-to-person" on all racial issues. In a large suburban school, for example, the one Black teacher was asked to moderate all conflicts involving the children of color in the school, to provide the resources for Black history month and to serve as the chairperson for diversity related events. Expected to be the "expert" on a range of racial issues, she also had to deal with the various feelings staff had about these issues.

Although the mission statements of many schools assert the value of diversity or difference, it is an open question how deeply such a statement penetrates into daily practice. Is it reflected in hiring? How do you ensure you have a diverse pool of teachers? What is the culture and climate of the organization? Who hangs around the lunchroom chatting? Who participates in informal social events? How is conflict handled? What are the organization's folk theories or common sense about race? Mission statements can function as empty platitudes or sources of ironic humor for community members of color who feel excluded or undervalued in multiple ways.

Acknowledging Race, Sharing Power, and Resources

As educators, while it is important to know who our students are, where they and their families come from, what life experiences they bring, it is equally important to know ourselves. What knowledge and experience do we bring to daily interactions, what expectations about the world? How do we accept children and/or parents who do things differently than we do? Can we avoid defining difference as deviance? As a student advisor explained to me once, it can be intimidating for a White person in a group of mostly Latino or Black peers if a different interactional style is in effect. The question is, is that kind of experience used as an opportunity to think about one's own cultural specificity, or is it used as an opening to vilify others as too raucous, too loud or inappropriate?

Along multiple dimensions, we are all constantly identifying in-groups and out-groups—those who are like us and those who are different. Research in cognitive psychology demonstrates that all of us "see" race, we are not colorblind (Crosby, Bromley, & Saxe, 1980; Dovidio, et al., 1997; Dovidio, et al., 2001; Vanman, et al., 1997). In addition, our "seeing" is not neutral. How would our practices change if we assumed race was, at some conscious or unconscious level, shaping our thinking about and interactions with others, if we assumed the need to be thoughtful? Asserting that "we are all the same" is not an effective way to avoid racial conflict. We all are different from each other in ways that are consequential and in ways that are useful. In fact, diversity can be an important resource for learning, productivity, and innovation in organizations. In amicus briefs in support of University of Michigan in the case of *Grutter v. Bollinger*, both leaders of major Fortune 500 companies and current and past leaders in all branches of the national defense all conveyed the value of having a diverse workforce: "*Amici* need the talent and creativity of a workforce that is as diverse as the world around it."[2] Such diversity brings a variety of strengths, skills, and perspectives. The point is not merely to tolerate difference but to learn to embrace it.

There is no way to "do" race correctly. But we can be assured trouble develops when we think racial dynamics are not present in our schools, when we think race is as something that we need worry about only when Black or Latino students are in the room, or only during February (Black History Month). Even if our goal is eventually to reach a place as a society where race matters less in our daily lives, there is no way to get there without paying significant attention to its current effects. If we continue to avoid difficult discussions about race and ignore the racial patterns in our organizational structures, processes and outcomes, the costs may be highest to children like Larry but all of us, even unwittingly, will play a role in perpetuating a too unequal racial status quo.

Notes

1. For an excellent elaboration of these points see the following web sites: http://raceandgenomics.ssrc.org/, www.pbs.org/race or http://raceproject.aaanet.org/
2. Brief for Amici Curiae 65 Leading American Businesses in Support of Respondents, Nos. 02-241 and 02-516 filed with the U.S. Supreme Court in *Grutter v. Bollinger*, February 18, 2003, p. 6.

References

Ainsworth-Darnell, J. W., & Downey, D. (1998). Assessing the oppositional culture explanation for racial/ethnic differences in school performance. *American Sociological Review*, 63, 536–553.

Allport, G. W. (1958). *The nature of prejudice*. Garden City, NY: Doubleday & Company.

American Anthropological Association. (1998). Statement on "race." Retrieved December 1, 2006, from http://www.aaanet.org/stmts/racepp.htm

Angier, N. (2000, August 22). Do races differ? Not really, genes show. New York Times. Retrieved August 23, 2000, from http://www.nytimes.com/library/national/science/082200 sci-genetics-race.html

Ayres, I., & Siegelman, P. (1995). Race and gender discrimination in bargaining for a new car. *American Economic Review*, 85, 304–321.

Begley, S. (1995, February 13). Three is not enough: Surprising new lessons from the controversial science of race. *Newsweek*, 67–69.

Bertrand, M., & Mullainathan, S. (2004). Are Emily and Greg More employable than Lakisha and Jamal? A field experiment on labor market discrimination. *American Economic Review*, 94, 991–1013.

Bobo, L., Kluegel, J. R., & Smith, R. A. (1997). Laissez faire racism: The crystallization of a "kinder, gentler" anti-black ideology. In S. A. Tuch & J. K. Martin (Eds.), *Racial attitudes in the 1990s: Continuity and change* (pp. 15–42). Westport, CT: Praeger.

Bonilla-Silva, E. (2003). *Racism without racists*. Lanham, MD: Rowman & Littlefield.

Carter, P. (2005). *Keepin' it real: School success beyond black and white*. New York: Oxford University Press.

Conley, D. (1999). *Being black, living in the red: Race, wealth, and social policy in America*. Berkeley: University of California Press.

Crenshaw, K. W. (1997). Color-blind dreams and racial nightmares: Reconfiguring racism in the post-civil rights era. In T. Morrison & C. Lacour (Eds.), *Birth of a nation'hood* (pp. 97–168). New York: Pantheon Books.

Crosby, F., Bromley, S. & Saxe, L. (1980). Recent unobtrusive studies of black and white discrimination and prejudice: A literature review. *Psychological Bulletin, 87*, 546–563.

Davis, F. J. (1991). *Who is black?: One nation's definition.* University Park: Pennsylvania State University Press.

Dovidio, J., Kawakami, K., Johnson, C., Johnson, B., & Howard, A. (1997). On the nature of prejudice: Automatic and controlled processes. *Journal of Experimental Social Psychology, 33*, 510–540.

Dovidio, J. F., Kawakani, K., & Beach K.R. (2001). Implicit and Explicit Attitudes: Examination of the Relationshnip Between Measures of Intergroup Bias. In R. Brown & S. L. Gaertner, (Eds.), *Blackwell Handbook of Social Psychology: Intergroup Processes* (pp 175–97). Malden, MA: Blackwell.

Feagin, J. R. (2001). *Racist America: Roots, current realities, and future reparations.* New York: Routledge.

Fish, S. (1993, November). Reverse racism, or how the pot got to call the kettle black. *Atlantic Monthly,* 1–10.

Fordham, S., & Ogbu, J. U. (1986). Black students' school success: Coping with the "burden of acting white." *Urban Review, 18*, 176–206.

Forman, T. (2004). Color-blind racism and racial indifference: The role of racial apathy in facilitating enduring inequalities. In M. Krysan & A. E. Lewis (Eds.), *Changing terrain of race & ethnicity* (pp. 43–66). New York: Russell Sage.

Forman, T., & Lewis, A. E. (2006). Racial apathy and hurricane Katrina: The social anatomy of prejudice in the post-civil rights era. *Du Bois Review, 3*, 175–202.

Gallagher, C. A. (2003). Color blind privilege: The social and political functions of erasing the color line in post-race America. *Race, Gender, & Class, 10*, 22–37.

Graves, J. (2001). *The emperor's new clothes: Biological theories of race at the millennium.* New Brunswick, NJ: Rutgers University Press.

Guglielmo, T. (2003). *White on arrival.* New York: Oxford University Press.

Haney-Lopez, I. (1996). *White by law: The legal construction of race.* New York: New York University Press.

Holt, T. C. (1995). Marking: Race, race-making, and the writing of history. *American Historical Review, 100*, 1–20.

Horvat, E., & O'Connor, C. (2006). *Beyond acting white: Reassessments and new directions in research on black students and school success.* Boulder, CO: Rowman & Littlefield.

Jackman, M. R. (1994). *The velvet glove: Paternalism and conflict in gender, class and race relations.* Berkeley: University of California Press.

Jacobson, M. F. (1998). *Whiteness of a different color: European immigrants and the alchemy of race.* Cambridge, MA: Harvard University Press.

Johnson, H. B. (2006). *The American dream and the power of wealth: Choosing schools and inheriting inequality in the land of opportunity.* New York: Routledge.

Johnson, H. B., & Shapiro, T. (2003). Good neighborhoods, good schools: Race and the "good choices" of white families. In A. W. Doane & E. Bonilla-Silva (Eds.), *White out: The continuing significance of race* (pp. 173–188). New York: Routledge.

Katznelson, I. (2005). *When affirmative action was white: An untold history of racial inequality in twentieth-century America.* New York: W.W. Norton.

Lareau, A. (2003). *Unequal childhoods.* Berkeley: University of California Press.

Lewis, A. E. (2001). There is no "race" in the schoolyard: Colorblind ideology in an (almost) all white school. *American Educational Research Journal, 38,* 781–812.

Lewis, A. E. (2003). *Race in the schoolyard: Negotiating the color line in classrooms and communities.* New Brunswick, NJ: Rutgers University Press.

Lewis, A. E. (2004). What group? Studying whites and whiteness in the era of colorblindness. *Sociological Theory, 22,* 623–646.

Lieber, M. (1994, October 23). An anthropological look at race and intelligence. *Chicago Tribune,* 3.

Lipsitz, G. (1998). *The possessive investment in whiteness: How white people profit from identity politics.* Philadelphia: Temple University Press.

Massey, D., & N. Denton. (1993). *American apartheid: Segregation and the making of the underclass.* Cambridge, MA: Harvard University Press.

O'Connor, C. (1997). Dispositions toward (collective) struggle and educational resilience in the inner city: A case analysis of six African-American high school students. *American Educational Research Journal, 34,* 593–629.

O'Connor, C. (1999). Race, class, and gender in America: Narratives of opportunity among low-income African American youths. *Sociology of Education, 72,* 137–157.

O'Connor, C., Horvat, E., & Lewis, A. (2006). Framing the field: Past and future research on the historic underachievement of black students. In. E. Horvat & C. O'Connor (Eds.), *Beyond acting white: Reassessments and new directions in research on black students and school success.* Boulder, CO: Rowman & Littlefield.

Oliver, M. L., & Shapiro, T. M. (1995). *Black wealth/White wealth: A new perspective on racial inequality.* New York: Routledge.

Omi, M., & Winant, H. (1994). *Racial formation in the United States: From the 1960s to the 1990s* (2nd ed.). New York: Routledge.

Pager, D., & Quillian, L. (2005). Walking the talk? What employers say versus what they do. *American Sociological Review, 70,* 355–380.

Payne, C. M. (1984). *Getting what we ask for: The ambiguity of success and failure in urban education* (Vol. 12). Westport, CT: Greenwood Press.

Roediger, D. R. (1991). *The wages of whiteness: Race and the making of the American working class.* New York: Verso.

Saporito, S., & Lareau, A. (1999). School selection as a process: The multiple dimensions of race in framing educational choice. *Social Problems, 46,* 418–439.

Schuman, H., Singer, E., Donovan, R., & Sellitz, C. (1983). Discriminatory behavior in New York restaurants. *Social Indicators Research, 13,* 69–83.

Shapiro, T. (2005). Race, Homeownership and Wealth. *Journal of Law and Policy* 20(53): 53–74.

Steele, C. M. (1999, August). Thin ice: "Stereotype Threat" and black college students. *Atlantic Monthly,* 44–54.

Turner, M., Fix, M., & Struyk, R. (1991). *Opportunities denied, opportunities diminished.* Washington, DC: Urban Institute Press.

Tyson, K. (2002). Weighing in: Elementary-age students and the debate on attitudes toward school among black students. *Social Forces, 80,* 1157–1189.

Tyson, K., Darity, W., & Castellino, D. (2005). It's not "a black thing": Understanding the burden of acting white and other dilemmas of high achievement. *American Sociological Review, 70,* 582–605.

Vanman, E. J., Paul, B. Y., Ito, T. A., & L Miller, Norman. (1997). The modern face of prejudice and structural features that moderate the effect of cooperation on affect. *Journal of Personality and Social Psychology, 73*(5): 941–959.

Wolff, E. N. (2001). *Racial wealth disparities: Is the gap closing?* New York: Levy Economics Institute of Bard College.

Yinger, J. (1995). *Closed doors, opportunities lost.* New York: Russell Sage.

· 4 ·

FOR WHAT IT'S WORTH:
CIVIL RIGHTS AND THE PRICE
OF LITERACY

BOB FECHO & SARAH SKINNER

Like they all wanted to beat me up and stuff. Like one dude named [unclear], he didn't like me since I was in the sixth grade. He was like in the eighth grade and he was like a bully ... I was like in fifth grade, [when] I got [to elementary school], and then all the girls flocked to me. And one dude named Martin, he got jealous and stuff and he wanted to beat me up to show off and stuff. So, when I got to [Growing City High School] they kind of told the other people. And other people didn't like me because of that.

But I think I'm doing good without them. I don't need them because if I am around them ... even if they liked me, I wouldn't be doing [good in school] like I do now because ... like three of them, they didn't graduate this year and I don't want that to happen to me. It is the same stories that will repeat with me and my sister. She didn't graduate because she was kind of like a party animal, you know? She didn't [work hard] at school. So, I wanted my mom to be proud of me and stuff. That's why I didn't talk to those people.

This extended quote is taken from an interview with Jorge, a Mexican American, who, at the time of this study, was attending ninth grade in a small, but growing city in southeast United States. In this excerpt, Jorge is primarily discussing his relationship with his Latino peers, a relationship that is complex and a source of concern. Largely, he shunned and was shunned by other young Latinos, citing, on their part, jealousy for his way with young woman and, on his part, his need to excel in school. Whatever the reasons, and we suspect they are more complex than has been noted here, Jorge remained isolated from his Latino peers and, at least at times, had seen this already bruised relationship diminish from social exile to physical threat, if not actual bodily harm.

However, his relationship with other Latinos isn't the only one discussed here. Near the excerpt's end, Jorge provided some insight into how he saw himself in relation to his sister and his mother. Although we have other data suggesting that Jorge respected and cared for his sister, it's also evident in this text that he drew parallels between his Latino peers who didn't take school seriously and his sister's failure to graduate for the same reasons. Yet, determined not to be the "same stor[y]," Jorge indicated that his mother provided him with a sense of purpose. If for no other reason than to make her proud, Jorge was determined to graduate from high school, even if it meant ostracizing himself and/or being ostracized from his neighborhood compadres.

This chapter, like all the other chapters in this book, raises questions about what it means to see literacy as a civil right, as an expectation of living, learning, and seeking prosperity within a country that we still want to believe leans toward democratic ideals and the hope of some day becoming a practicing democracy, that is, the United States of America. Specifically, we ask what is the price of literacy as a civil right, is the same proportional tax levied on all, and who pays the bulk of the burden. Ultimately, we question whether the goods and services provided are worth the cost, particularly for those who need to pay the dearest price.

We examine these questions through the eyes, words, and experiences of Jorge, using his case as a means for access into larger discussions of these issues. We use the work of Bakhtin (1981), as well as that of two social psychologists— Hermans and Kempen (1993)—and four social anthropologists— Holland, Lachicotte, Skinner, and Cain (1998)—to focus our discussion and form a theoretical framework. Using this theoretical framework to transact with the particulars of Jorge's case, we wonder aloud about the questions we raised and, hopefully, enter into dialogue about what it means for literacy to be a right, whether or not we all have equitable access to that right, and, failing that, what we might do to achieve such access.

Theoretical Framework

In a Bakhtinian (1981) world, language remains constantly in flux, tugged between opposing tensions in a process he called heteroglossia, literally different tongues. In this process, centripetal forces pull language toward the center, always seeking stability and unification. Construed benignly, such forces foster communication because they allow large numbers of language users access to a language that remains constant and undergoes little change. However, at their most malevolent forms, such forces become the tools of oppressive regimes that, through control of the language, seek also to control flexibility of thought. Stripped of personality and fluidity, language becomes, as Bakhtin notes, a "dead, thing-like shell" (p. 355).

Conversely, the opposing force of heteroglossia is centrifugal in nature, urging language away from center toward variety and flexibility. In a positive light, centrifugal forces allow for a wide range of language users to find themselves in and have input into the language, creating a personal connection to language use. However, when too much individualism and flexibility occurs, the language loses commonalty, and the result is ever diminishing degrees of communication. The language becomes so closely identified with such a small group of speakers that it no longer fulfills the need for broad communication.

Ultimately, Bakhtin (1981) suggested that a healthy state of language exists at the point in which the centrifugal and centripetal forces intersect. As he noted, every speaking turn or writing task "serves as a point where centrifugal as well as centripetal forces are brought to bear," where they "intersect in the utterance" (p. 272). He elaborated that "[e]very utterance participates in the 'unitary language' (in its centripetal forces and tendencies) and at the same time partakes of social and historical heteroglossia (the centrifugal, stratifying forces)" (p. 272, parentheses in the original). The upshot of this transaction is that language remains in flux and, to an extent, in conflict. What individual words and words in combination mean are entirely dependent upon the context in which they are uttered or written. Understanding comes in response.

Using Bakhtin's concept of heteroglossia as a base, Hermans and Kempen (1993) argued that the self, primarily constructed through language, is a "highly contextual phenomenon" (p. 78) and remains constantly in flux. Who we are—for example, Mexican American, child of a working mother, adolescent male who has embraced literacy, brother, tennis player—is a complicated mix of selves that is presented as a whole in the social worlds we inhabit even as various identities within us dialogue. They further argued that power relations mark the transactions between self and social worlds, as well as among the many selves within us. They indicated that "[t]he more symmetrical the dialogue is, the more it provides opportunity for mutual influence; the more asymmetrical it is, the more it constrains the exchange of views and experiences" (p. 78). In short, who we are depends on where we are and how we have constructed ourselves to date.

Holland et al. (1998) have also used Bakhtin's work as a means for understanding identity, particularly as it transacts with agency. Specifically, they have noted what they call improvisations, placing much importance on these actions because "they tell us where—along the margins and interstices of collective cultural and social constructions—how, and with what difficulties human actors, individuals, and groups are able to redirect themselves" (p. 278). They remind us that Bakhtin holds that "the world must be answered— authorship is not a choice—but the form of the answer is not predetermined" (p. 272). There is an existential quality here (Fecho with Green, 2004; Gordon, 2000) that suggests, "if we are alive ... then we are engaged in answering what is directed to us" (Holland, et al., 1998, p. 279). It is through improvisation that humans enact agency, or that

> capacity ... to act purposively and reflectively ... to reiterate and remake the world in which they live, in circumstances where they may consider different courses of action possible and desirable, though not necessarily from the same point of view.

In doing so, one reorients one's behavior and helps to refigure a previously figured world, both individually and collectively. According to Holland et al. (1998), such a space "remains, more often than not, a contested space, a space of struggle" (p. 282).

In the remainder of this chapter, we look at the case of Jorge and use this theoretical framework as a foundation from which we make our argument. Most importantly, we want to bring our understanding of heteroglossia, the dialogic self, and improvisation to bear on the ways Jorge attempted to function as a learner within a high school in the northeast quadrant of Georgia. As Jorge moved across the social worlds of his peers, his family, the neighborhood, the classroom, and the larger culture of the school, he encountered different responses and authored different responses to this mesh of transactions. We offer a close examination of what these transactions meant for Jorge and, possibly, what they cost in the doing.

Particulars of the Study

Jorge's case is drawn from a larger study of the literacy attitudes of adolescent boys raised in working-class families. In searching for participants for his study, Bob asked teachers in area high schools to look for young men who had embraced literacy for their own purposes and whose parents worked in jobs that could be considered as working-class positions. By *working class*, he meant that they had jobs in the service, manufacturing, agriculture, or business industries for which they had little say as to their job description, the conditions of their employment, and the future direction of that business. By this definition, an electrician who ran his own business would not be considered working class, although an electrician who was employed by a manufacturing firm to service their machines would be. Jorge's mother, by virtue of her job working on the line in a car brake manufacturing plant, easily fell under our definition of working-class employment. Although how much money one makes and what one values certainly figure into any discussion of what counts as being of the working class, ultimately for us, a position for which a worker has little power over the circumstances of that position is frequently the deciding factor. Although we suspect there are readers who would contest this definition, we can't imagine any definition of *working class* that would stand uncontested.

We should also unpack our request for adolescent boys who *embrace literacy for their own purposes*. In offering further explanation to the teachers supporting his efforts, Bob explained that he was looking for young men who routinely read books and/or other print and electronic media and/or routinely wrote via traditional pen and paper media and/or electronic media as a means of making sense of their contexts and their identities and roles within those contexts. More briefly, they read or composed because they had needs to do so. In particular, they used their literacy skills beyond classroom assignments.

Historical Context and Purpose of the Study

This study has its origins in Bob's experience of growing up in Pennsylvania. His father worked in a car frame factory and his mother worked in various clothing manufacturing mills. The families that populated the neighborhood of brick row houses where he lived and went to school were decidedly working class, by our definition and most likely by any definition one could offer. But from the start of his formal education, unlike many of the boys in his neighborhood, Bob embraced reading and writing, and indulged himself whenever he wasn't doing chores or playing the rough and tumble games of the city block where he lived. Although he never felt completely connected to his boyhood neighborhood, he also felt separate from the children of professionals who dominated the college preparatory classes of his junior and high schools.

As an educator and researcher, he is acutely aware of what he has gained through his embracing of literacy and formal education, but is equally aware of what he has lost. Furthermore, although he feels that formal education has added to his life, he remains a critic of that very education. In particular, he argues that, too often, he learned in spite of and not because of the way he was taught, which was mostly various iterations of what Freire (1970) has called "the banking model" of education—teachers depositing information into his brain for future withdrawal via tests and quizzes. Consequently, as one strand of his research agenda, he has sought to understand what it meant to be a working-class male adolescent who had embraced literacy for his own purposes and was currently attending high schools.

Participants in and Context of the Study

To initiate the study, Bob recruited four area teachers—all teacher consultants with whom he had working relationships owing to their common involvement in the Red Clay Writing Project, a local site of the National Writing Project, a long established professional learning initiative. These teachers volunteered to participate in the study and were given the charge noted earlier. Beyond identifying students he could approach, the teachers' responsibilities were to act as liaisons among the students and their parents and Bob, and to be part of the data gathering team. They would send weekly e-mail vignettes about the student(s) whom they identified, discussing some event in the classroom that they felt gave insight into the student's literacy experience.

Having student referrals from these teachers, Bob contacted the students and their families and set up a face-to-face dialogue to explain the project. Six students were contacted and all six and their families agreed to their participation. The young men— Andy, Esteban, Isaac, Jorge, Kent, and Neil—were all high school students at the time of this study. Esteban and Jorge were Latinos who had both come to the United States after having lived part of their childhoods in Central America and Mexico, respectively. Both were in tenth grade at Growing City High School (GCHS) and were proficient enough in English to be interviewed and to take part in the e-mail discussions. Andy, a European American, also attended GCHS, but was a graduating senior hoping to go to college. Kent, also a European American, matriculated at Small Rural High School (SRHS) as a junior and, like Andy, was involved in athletics. Neil and Isaac, both European Americans, attended New Suburbia High School

(NSHS) with Neil finishing tenth grade and Isaac trying to gain enough senior credit to graduate.

The Data Set and Data Analysis

In addition to (a) the weekly e-mail vignettes sent by the identifying teachers, the data set, collected from January to May of 2004, consisted of (b) two 45–90 minute interviews—one at the start and one near the end of the data collection period—conducted individually with Andy, Isaac, Jorge, and Neil; (c) one 45–90 minute interview conducted individually with Esteban and Kent; (d) field notes of monthly observations of each student; (e) weekly listserv discussions among the students, frequently prompted by Bob; (f) weekly individual questions asked and responded to via e-mail; and (g) occasional writing artifacts volunteered by the young men. By capturing the experiences of these students through a variety of methods, media, and perspectives, Bob gained a data set that was triangulated and rich in possibility. To further add to the triangulation, Bob invited two graduate students—coauthor Sarah Skinner, as well as Kristi Amatucci—to help him analyze and report the data.

After multiple readings of the data, general themes were identified and more deeply investigated. These themes—currently identified as (a) measuring the gap between one's own and the dominant culture, (b) being centrifugal to an aspired to peer culture, (c) filling existential needs, and (d) improvising within social worlds—the three of us began to write the data (Richardson, 1994) as a means of further particularizing those themes for each case. Stated broadly, we identified the following understandings as being supported by the data:

1. The young men of this study, when embracing literacy, frequently did so at the cost of isolating themselves from their working-class peers and the more middle-class students of the school.
2. The more a young man in the study tried to identify with his aspired to peer culture (i.e., to see himself as belonging to a peer culture he aspired to), the less willing he was to admit to involvement in literacy practices, despite other evidence to the contrary.
3. The more a young man perceived himself to be different from the aspired to peer culture (i.e., to be more centrifugal than centripetal to that group) the more likely he would be reading and writing to make sense of that experience.

Limitations of this Study

This study is based on six case studies conducted in a limited amount of time—one semester. Like all case studies, it is unwise to make generalizations for large populations from them, although we would argue that such generalization holds true for all research. Regardless, there is no attempt in this chapter to argue that what we have come to understand about these six young men is the same for all working-class young men who have embraced literacy. That said, we do argue that the experiences detailed here and the understanding we derived from these experiences give us insight into the larger considerations of other young men who aspire to certain cultures and seek to make meaning through reading and writing.

Jorge's Case

For the purposes of this chapter, we focused on the experiences of Jorge, primarily because, of the six cases studied, his most dramatically resonated with the themes associated with this book. In particular, his case raises questions about who has easier and less costly access to literacy education and, for those with more restricted access, what does it mean for their personal construction of self. By highlighting Jorge's positioning in terms of the family that encourages him, the neighborhood in which he lives, the school he attends, and the students with whom he shares classrooms, we indicate the ways in which he improvised within and around those cultures while in pursuit of the education he valued, at least for the sake of his mother. We also raise questions as to the cost of that improvisation and what that implies for Jorge and others. Finally, although Jorge's case is situated in a study focused on issues of socioeconomic class, we can't deny and, indeed, comment on the ways his other cultural selves, particularly ethnicity, transact in his life.

Of Self, Identity, and Context

At the time of data collection, Jorge was a 14-year-old freshman living in a growing city in Georgia, along with his mother, his sister, and his sister's toddler. It was in this apartment that Bob first interviewed Jorge. In the poem that follows, Bob tried to gather a sense of that apartment complex, a sense formed as he pulled into the parking lot and climbed the stairs to the second floor. If, as Bakhtin (1981) suggested, all meaning is embedded in context, it is key for those of us who conduct research to have rich invokings of context and what such context implies for our understandings.

Our choice to use a poem to convey the context comes from this need on our parts to create a more vivid sense of the context and, in particular, develop a more metaphoric understanding of Jorge in relation to his surroundings. Bob originally wrote this poem to help him—raised in cities in northeast United States—to gain some deeper sense of the context in which Jorge was living. However, given that many who might read this chapter neither come from nor currently live in such contexts, we decided to include it here so that all readers might gain more proximity to this space of interesting contrasts.

Cinderblocks
stacked
one on the other
forming two stories
Cement stairs
metal-reinforced
with open risers
zig zag
to the narrow ledge
that runs the length
Steel door
first on the left
painted like red clay
after a rain
stings my knuckles
as I knock
Car wheels grumble
on the gravel lot
Eyes
suspicious or disbelieving
watch me
from across the way
Chains clatter
undone from inside
and the door groans open
Warmth flows out
the rigid frame
into the twilight chill
and voices
softly rounding syllables

pull me through
to where
neons swim in
turquoise water
An incandescent glow
lights the living room kitchen
The TV murmurs
A wide-eyed baby coos
from the welcoming lap
of a smiling woman
Framed on the wall
the awards of childhood
(Where are mine
In boxes maybe)
celebrate the future
through the past

Although Bob saw the apartment complex as somewhat stark, Jorge and his family had fashioned a warm sense of a home inside. It was from this vantage point that Jorge sought and conducted his American education, an education that manifested itself in a number of ways. Having been part of the local school system's English for Speakers of Other Languages (ESOL) program since the sixth grade, Jorge had recently tested out of the program and was looking forward, but not without some trepidation, to mainstream courses at GCHS. He was an industrious, if erratic, student and had been recognized for his promise by being invited for two consecutive terms to the local university's Hispanic Youth Leadership Camp. Possessing a passion for tennis, which he learned through television and practicing alone against a wall, he was the only Latino member of the school's tennis team. This passion distanced him from many of his Latino peers, who if they were involved in sports, chose to be members of the school's soccer team. In addition, according to one of his teachers, he played the piano, which further separated him from other Latino teenagers at the school.

Jorge claimed to "enjoy learning at school," but he also recognized that the Internet and other modes of technology—like television—offered him means for education as well. He took advantage of these resources, building his language skills along with his sense of style, including his style of dress. "I don't like to dress like a lot of Hispanic people because … when I go places people mistreat me because of my Hispanic reputation." He claimed to avoid the baggy jeans and extra-long shirts, what he described as the "Latino look," and which he felt was embraced and showcased by his Latino peers at school.

Instead, he wore primarily chinos and polo shirts, dress more akin to the tennis team we suspect.

Fully understanding the role that his education would play in attaining his professional dreams and goals, Jorge wanted to do well in school in order to become a lawyer or a tennis pro. However, knowing the difficulties he might encounter in achieving these dreams, Jorge, in somewhat of a pragmatic and perhaps fallback stance, had also voiced an interest in a career as an electrician. We see this creation of B & C plans as somewhat typical of working-class youth who seek careers in the professional sector. In Bob's experience, he remembers wishing to study to be a writer of fiction or perhaps an architect, but then, as he thought at the time, "settled" for teaching. Although he no longer feels he settled and has found a home for himself in education, a pervasive reason for choosing teaching was that, having known teachers, but not knowing writers or architects, he could more easily imagine becoming the former but neither of the latter. We suspected in the case of Jorge that, although the athletic life of a tennis pro or the professional status of a career in law seemed inviting, the possibility of becoming an electrician seemed much more reachable, especially given the sense of conflict and alienation he felt already as a young Latino seeking to achieve in high school.

When we consider Jorge's home context, we intuit the presence of strong centripetal tensions at play. There is an admitted desire on his part to enter mainstream culture, as is evidenced by his dress, his sport of choice, and his aspirations. In fact, if we were to consider this home context alone, our understandings of Jorge would be skewed along the lines of observing primarily a willingness on his part to buy into the mainstream culture in large ways. However, centrifugal tensions are also always at play, and the next sections will investigate how these forces transacted with his sense of the self and the ability to act on his own behalf.

Of Family, Community, and Heteroglossia

One of our intents of the earlier poem was to convey a sense of a rich home life, one that—despite compactness of the space in which it occurred—resonated with depth and warmth. An understanding of Jorge's academic motivations and choices begins with an understanding of how he saw himself connected to his family, particularly his mother. These connections began with a conception of pride in his heritage. Born and raised in a small town in Mexico, as were his mother and father, Jorge noted proudly that his grandfather came from Spain.

He seemed to understand the power of heritage and its connection to culture, and he had great appreciation for these connections. He also had come to realize that he, too, played a part in carrying on traditions of pride worthy of his family's heritage. He wanted to continue or extend the narrative already created by his family's past, metaphorically writing his own chapter to his family's history.

As Jorge wrote in response to online questions, his education began "outside school because there was a lot of history to [listen to] from my grandmother." Her stories, delivered orally owing to her lack of formal education, became a source of learning for Jorge. He claimed that "the only good teacher that I had was my grandmother. She teach me history because [of her] stories." In many ways, the heard narrative became the script through which Jorge negotiated his future understandings and part of the means by which he measured his own actions. Although his grandmother was not able to read and write, Jorge had other family members living in the same building who provided access to books. In addition, at least one cousin had attended a technical college, serving somewhat to develop Jorge's appreciation for formal schooling.

Originally starting school in Mexico and increasing his degree of literacy before entering school, Jorge stated that he learned to read in Spanish during first grade. Regarding his early literacy, he wrote:

> When I was a young child I din't write much but if I writte it would be in Spnish. I din't copy sentences from the board, unless I was ask too, but otherwise I din't. Sometimes I write some of the feelings and toughts that came true my mind. Some times I was ashamed of my toughts so I dnn't wrote them down. I din't worried about how I writte or use penmanship.

Therefore, Jorge came to the United States literate in Spanish and old enough to be aware of his mother's aspirations for him. Seeking better economic and educational opportunities for her family, Jorge's mother had left him in the care of his grandmother and immigrated to the United States and eventually Georgia, where she worked nights manufacturing car brakes. Sent for by his mother after a three-year separation, Jorge came, along with his sister, to live with his mother in their small apartment.

For Jorge, an education, including solid reading and writing skills, was necessary to repay the debt he owed to his mother for her efforts, both in coming to America and in continuing to provide for him. Specifically, he openly stated that his education and learning were important because they were a means for him to "help my family," to contribute to their income and well-being. His sense of needing to do well for the sake of his mother was a continuing theme throughout his face-to-face interviews and online responses. This sense of debt extended to his own adolescent urges to succumb to both mass media advertising and peer pressure as he continued to place additional burdens on his mother to provide luxury items that, although they furthered his entry into a more mainstream lifestyle, placed a financial toll upon the family. As he wrote online:

> Offten I make my mom to buy me [stuff] that I dont even need and dont use. Almost all the time I reflect on what I have done (make my mom buy [me stuff]) so I [feel] bad because every day I see my mom caming from work verry tired, just to buy me things that I don't need.

Jorge's desires for material goods and comforts created a sense of guilt when seen in the light of his mother's struggles to make ends meet. Although other teenagers, even those in mainstream families, might also experience remorse after making material demands of tired and overworked parents, Jorge's guilt was enhanced by his heightened self-awareness of his role in adding to that burden.

From our data, it appears that education remained the paramount vehicle for fulfillment of the social and economic aspirations of Jorge and his family. He particularly put emphasis on his writing skills because, as he wrote, he "would like to be a lawyer and they have to do a lot of writing" and "because laws change all the time, I never stop learning because every day I learn different things from small to big things." He viewed his literacy and education as a means to pay homage to his heritage and those who came before him. Overall, though, he positioned himself as a lifelong learner, again showing his understanding of the fluidity of his position and identity, but claiming this positioning as another means to make his mother proud of him.

In these excerpts, we identified a stronger sense of opposing tensions at play. Despite his not wanting to "dress Latino"—whatever that might mean—Jorge's embrace of modern U.S. culture remained in tension with his respect for his Mexican and Spanish heritage. To date, his grandmother remained his "best teacher," and his will to achieve in school was directly linked to expectations and examples set by his mother. The foundations for literacy were laid down in Mexican schools. Yet, the key to achievement in U.S. schools, as indicated by Delpit (1995), Nieto (2002), and others, is to be aware of, critical of, and also fluent in the mainstream power codes. Jorge seemed aware of and moved toward fluency in these codes, yet appeared from our data less critical of what such awareness and fluency might mean. Without that critique, the education that Jorge sought at the behest of his mother was a centripetal force that had the potential to separate him from his heritage and family.

Of School, Peers, and Improvisation

The closeness Jorge felt for his family was not replicated in the neighborhood or at school, places where he purposefully distanced himself from others his own age. He consciously opted not to associate with other male adolescents in his neighborhood because "they all get into fights and gangs and my mom kept me out of them ... and one time they shot like people over there (pointing in the direction of a far corner of the apartment complex) and so I never went back there." Rather than risk other teens negatively affecting his goals, he opted for isolation.

This somewhat self-imposed isolation carried over to school. Described by his ESOL teacher, Elder, as "generally a loner when he works," Jorge, despite his aspirations, was an inconsistent learner in her classroom, at times "articulate and funny" and at times having trouble "getting out what I know he wants to say." She further described him as "kind of quirky," worrying that "he is always separate from other students." She was also concerned at his seeming disengagement at times in class, writing, "He sits in his desk and stretches his crossed legs out in front of him and crosses his arms across his chest. He looks off into space and doesn't always make eye contact with you when he is speaking." Although Elder suggested that Jorge could be a class clown at times, he spent more time trying to fall under her gaze, organizing her things and sitting close to her, seeming to desire her attention and appreciation. However, she also commented that there were times when he was shy and withdrawn, adding, "He seems to like attention and at the same time distance[d] himself from attention."

At lunch, Jorge elected to sit with the Latinas from his classes rather than boys his own age: "I just don't get along with the boys. They think they are the popular dudes ... They don't like me, I guess [pause] I'm smarter than them, that's why." Reasoning that jealousy over what he construed as his academic achievement and seriousness toward education made him a target for ridicule, Jorge removed himself from the spaces in which that teasing could readily occur, using the Latinas as a buffer against the taunts and aggression that might come his way in the less supervised confines of a high school cafeteria.

This isolation continued in his ESOL classes, where he appeared unable to find male peers with whom he could form relationships. For example, Esteban, another Latino in Jorge's class and also a participant in this study, served more as a source of conflict rather than a means of companionship. Elder remarked, "There is some definite tension between Jorge and Esteban in my class" and, from our observations, the two rarely spoke to each other during informal classroom moments. Perhaps this distancing stemmed from the two boys' varying perspectives on school and the class, for as Jorge took his assignments more seriously—particularly when his grades were in danger—Esteban was more interested in other things. According to Elder, Esteban "wastes a lot of time ... [and] is interested in a lot of other things other than school. He flirts with girls and tries to make people laugh." Although gifted in language study and, to our casual assessment, somewhat more accomplished than Jorge in his acquisition of English to that moment, Esteban longed to be the center of the class's attention and frequently downplayed his obvious facility with language. Jorge, as we noted, was more interested in the teacher's attention rather than that from his peers. The upshot remained that, although he asserted he was fine with the arrangement, Jorge had little positive interaction with Latinos his own age and, we suspect, school must have made him feel lonely, if not fully isolated, at times.

Distanced from other young Latinos, Jorge was also not embraced by the mainstream Anglo population. His position as a second-language learner frequently earned him ridicule from many of the other students at school, particularly concerning what he construed as his strong Spanish accent and his pronunciation of certain words. As he noted in an interview:

> People make fun of me, like in my social studies class, there is not a single person that has never repeat what I say ... everybody will say something that I say funny ... they all make fun of me.

Furthermore, even his tennis teammates "made a lot of fun of me since I'm the only Hispanic on the team and they had a chance to pick on me," especially after he lost several matches. However, the team teasing seemed to lessen when he gained confidence in his skills and began to win more. He professed that he handled his peers' teasing by ignoring it, saying, "What goes in that ear, comes out the other ear. I don't really care."

Regardless, he had not found any real friends or confidants among his teammates or his classmates, whether a part of the ESOL program or the mainstream population. He claimed that he was not lonely without any best friends and that he was content with being alone. As he reiterated in an interview:

> I think I'm doing good without [friends]. I don't need them ... I see all of those people ... they didn't graduate this year and I don't want that to happen to me ... I wanted my mom to be proud of me and stuff.

Rather than risk succumbing to negative peer relations that could damage his educational opportunities or deter him from his long-range goals, he positioned himself in isolation and perceived safety. For Jorge, his distancing from peers was not viewed as a sacrifice, yet he was nonetheless forced into such isolation owing to his otherness as a second-language learner, as a child of the working class, as a Latino, and as a young male who embraced literacy.

Yet again, Jorge found himself as the flag in an educational tug of war with the stability of mainstream education tugging him centripetally and the companionship of peers so craved by adolescents pulling him in centrifugal ways. Although Jorge's inclinations fell toward the latter, it didn't necessarily bring him acceptance. Instead, what we saw here was Jorge's attempts to improvise a space for himself somewhat adjacent to the communities with which he routinely transacted. Neither fully fitting into the neighborhood nor finding a place among the mainstream population, Jorge had established buffer zones—the lunchroom Latinas, his family's apartment, classroom space, his tennis game—to help him run the gauntlet of personal attacks that he experienced on a near daily basis. To minimize the impact of these mostly verbal attacks, he had constructed ways to both physically and emotionally distance himself from the instigators. That insulation was purchased, at least to our belief, through isolation, and at a fairly high price.

Implications

Although we wrote explicitly about Jorge—and, through inference, about other students like him—this chapter, in many ways, is also about the other Latinos from whom Jorge remained estranged. The questions raised here not only affect those who seek to conform to the school's mainstream culture but also those who question the need to conform. If literacy is a civil right, why is that right "purchased" at different rates of exchange for different students, and why do those rates of exchange seem to be more costly for those further removed from the mainstream culture. In addition, why are students like Jorge, who are willing to pay that rate of exchange, fewer in number, while others—those who, like Jorge indicated, didn't graduate—are seeming to grow in numbers? Whether due to his family's support, his own sense of agency, a strong belief in an American education, or a combination of these and other factors, Jorge had opted to accept a life that to us appeared isolated and lonely in exchange for a perceived path toward success in a future career. Yet, as graduation rates

If literacy is a civil right, we need a literacy that gets beyond the rote skill and drill of phonics, decoding, and comprehension. Instead we need literacy instruction and practice that encourage students to explore the range of expression available to them; to consider the ways their home, neighborhood, and mainstream codes transact; to delve into the consequences, both immediate and long term, of language choice in their lives; to call into question the mainstream codes even as it provides them with deliberate access to those codes; to make meaning of the marginalization that seems to randomly enter the lives of too many people in this country; to use their abilities to read and write to forge new lines of understandings for themselves, their communities, and the larger society around them.

To teach literacy as we have just outlined is to teach literacy as a means for existential exploration, as a way of granting all students access to literacy that is critical and enables them to make more complex meaning of their lives in relation to the mainstream culture. Without such a stance on teaching, Latino and working-class young men in general will continue to drop out of school because they will fail to see the agency that might exist if they continue in school, but use their growing literacy to call their language education into question. Moreover, others like Jorge will remain, but will run the risk of assimilating rather than engaging language, of inhabiting worlds in which they have little voice, and of reifying the myth of literacy as the mother of capitalist success stories. Neither choice is acceptable.

References

Bakhtin, M. (1981). Discourse in the novel. In Holquist, M (Ed.), *The dialogic imagination* (C. Emerson & M. Holquist, Trans.) (pp. 259–422). Austin: University of Texas Press.

Delpit, L. (1995). *Other people's children: Cultural conflict in the classroom.* New York: New Press.

Fecho, B. (2004). *"Is this English?" Race, language, and culture in the classroom.* New York: Teachers College Press.

Fecho, B. with Green, A. (2004). Learning with Aaron. In B. Fecho (Ed.), *"Is this English?" Race, language, and culture in the classroom* (pp. 91–112). New York: Teachers College Press.

Freire, P. (1970). *Pedagogy of the oppressed.* New York: Continuum.

Fry, R. (2005, November 1). *Recent changes in the entry of Hispanic and white youth into college.* Retrieved September 15, 2006, from http://pewhispanic.org/reports/report. php?ReportID=56

Gee, J. P. (1996). *Social linguistics and literacies: Ideology in discourses.* London: Routledge Falmer.

Gordon, L. (2000). *Existentia Africana: Understanding Africana, existential thought.* New York: Routledge.

Greene, J. P. (2002). *High school graduation rates in the United States*. Retrieved September 15, 2006, from http://www.torres4bpt.com/pdf/cr_baeo.pdf

Hermans, H. & Kempen, H. (1993). *The dialogical self: Meaning as movement*. San Diego, CA: Academic Press.

Holland, D., Lachicotte, W., Skinner, D., & Cain, C. (1998). *Identity and agency in cultural worlds*. Cambridge, MA: Harvard University Press.

Nieto, S. (2002). *Language, culture, and teaching: Critical perspectives for a new century*. Mahwah, NJ: Lawrence Erlbaum Associates.

Pew Hispanic Center. (2004, January). *National survey of Latinos: Education*. Retrieved September 15, 2006, from http://pewhispanic.org/files/factsheets/7.pdf

Richardson, L. (1994). Writing: A method of inquiry. In N. K. Densin & Y. S. Lincoln (Eds.), *Handbook of qualitative research* (pp. 516–529). Thousand Oaks, CA: Sage.

· 5 ·

THE WAGES OF WHITENESS? RETHINKING ECONOMIC METAPHORS FOR WHITENESS: LITERACY AND LIFE GOALS IN AN ALL-WHITE SUBURBAN HIGH SCHOOL

JENNIFER SEIBEL TRAINOR

Laura[1] is a senior at an all-White suburban high school located twenty miles from a mid-sized, mid-Eastern city. A straight "A" student, with two Advanced Placement (AP) courses under her belt, she lives in a gated community in a large home with her parents and younger brother. Like virtually all of her peers at this public school, Laura is White. We are sitting in her Advanced Writing course, an elective for college-bound seniors, waiting for the bell to ring. I ask her about her postgraduation plans:

> I'll probably go to State [a local college with a noncompetitive admissions policy]. I got into Northwestern though, and I really thought I might go there. My parents have saved for a long time for me to go to college, and they are real encouraging. They went to college, and like, they know it was important. But I know if I go somewhere expensive, it will be harder for them to pay for my brother, and they have to think about his college, in two years, you know? I don't want to put that kind of burden on them. But my dad, he's like, Laura, it's your decision. We support you. But you know, it's ridiculous to spend that kind of money when you don't have to. It's like, you can get the same education at a place like State. And honestly, it will be nicer for my mom, if I stay around here, even live at home. We're real close, and it would be hard for her, to be so far away.

I turn to her classmate, James, also White. His father and brother both have bachelor's degrees from nearby universities.

"What are your plans for next year?" I ask, "Are you applying for college?"

"No," he says, drawing out the word in an embarrassed shrug. "I don't think so. I'm not, like, 'college material' or whatever, you know? I'm not good at school. I just want to get a job, and you can get good jobs without going to college. I might go to Western Valley [a local two-year technical school], and they'll teach you like, about cars or computers. My cousin did that, and he makes a lot of money now, and has his own apartment."

In *Literacy and Racial Justice: The Politics of Learning after Brown v. Board of Education*, Catherine Prendergast (2003) argues that "throughout American history literacy has been managed and controlled in myriad ways to rationalize and ensure White domination" and that Whites have been "willing to commit crimes large and small in order to maintain their exclusive franchise on ... literacy institutions" (p. 5). Indeed, she argues, Whites have an "investment in literacy" and hence one of the key components of the ideology of literacy—the collective beliefs about its definition, purpose, and utility—has been the notion that literacy and its institutions, including schools and universities, belong to Whites. Prendergast's analysis, particularly the economic language she uses to describe the relationship between Whiteness and literacy (Whites have a "franchise on" and "investment in" literacy and its institutions) derives from Critical Race Theory (CRT) and its lexicon of economic metaphors for Whiteness. Critical Race Theorists liken Whiteness to a wage, property, or investment (see, for example, Roediger, 1991; Lipsitz 1998). Cheryl Harris (1991) explains the power of the metaphor succinctly: "Whiteness ... meets the functional criteria of property. Specifically, the law has accorded 'holders' of Whiteness the same privileges and benefits accorded holders of other types of property" (p. 1731).

One of the privileges of Whiteness, of course, is education. As Gloria Ladson-Billings and William Tate (1995) note, if Whiteness is property, then we need to consider the role of Whiteness in education, as "property relates to education in explicit and implicit ways." Those with "better property," Ladson-Billings and Tate write, "are entitled to 'better' schools" (pp. 53–54). Thus, school inequality may be a literal matter of property-tax funding, but it is also a matter of race privilege and the power of Whiteness to "entitle" one to "better" schools. Recent ethnographies of schooling document the racial dimensions of the competitive struggle to ensure continued White ownership of schooling. For example, Denise Clark Pope (2001) describes a high school situated in an affluent California suburb, a place where nearly all of the students graduate and attend prestigious universities. It is a place, in Pope's words, where people are "obsessed" with being the best, and with helping their children acquire top credentials. "The drive to succeed," she writes, "has led some parents to employ expensive agencies to tutor their children to get high scores on the SATs ... Other families turn to web sites that sell high-priced college application essays guaranteed to get students into ivy league schools" (pp. 166–167). At a gathering of local third graders, Pope notes that the children speak in earnest of their hopes to attend Stanford or Harvard when they grow up. "I want to be rich and drive a Lexus" a youngster remarks. "So I need to get A's in school" (p. 167). Pope describes the effects—in terms of intellectual and moral development, as well as physical and mental health—of these students' struggle to cash in on their ownership of literacy.

Although not all of the focal students in Pope's study are White, and although Pope attempts to bracket race out of her discussion (it is "beyond the scope" of her study, she writes in a footnote), the racial dimensions of "doing school" are apparent to the students of color she talks to. About one of her Latina focal students, for example, Pope writes:

> Teresa perceives a difference in the way the white and Mexican students are treated at school. She associates qualities such as whiteness, wealth, and power (at least power over the school curriculum) with the students who live in the suburbs. She sees some sort of connection between the amount of taxes one pays and an ability to influence school decisions such as who teaches and what material is taught in school programs. She is convinced that the honors program and other programs where "white" students are well represented are "better" because "white parents" want to ensure that their kids get into college and will "make sure" the program is "good." (p. 78)

Teresa's perceptions about the connections between race, privilege, and schooling suggest that White ownership of literacy is embedded in layers of school practices (honors programs, curricular choices, school funding), and in concomitant decisions about who is included in particular programs and who is not. It also suggests that the manipulation and cheating that Pope documents are raced activities, that "doing school"—what she defines as manipulating school to maximize one's own advantage—participates in perpetuating racism and racial domination.

Brantlinger (2003) describes this domination in her ethnographic study of middle-class parents' involvement in school. As Brantlinger writes, "White members of the professional class" work to "secure the best of what schools have to offer for [their] own children" (p. xi). In her study, Brantlinger describes White parents who exert considerable influence on school practices by pressuring school personnel to put their preferences into effect (p. 58). For these parents, "children's school success is part of a status competition among parents," and they thus preferred, and worked to maintain, segregated and stratified schools that benefited middle-class students. Both of these studies, Brantlinger's in particular, remind us that literacy is yet another invisible advantage in the "knapsack of White privilege," to borrow Peggy McIntosh's phrase (1992), a commodity that Whites can cash in on by the simple virtue of being White.

But consider for a moment that most students in the United States do not, upon graduation from high school, attend elite, selective admissions four-year institutions. Consider what John Alberti (2001) calls a major class division in American higher education: the gap between first-tier selective admissions schools and second-tier open registration, regional two- and four-year colleges—he calls "working class" colleges (p. 565). These schools, not elite, competitive universities, comprise the majority of institutions of higher education in the United States. Many of them are distinctly vocational in orientation. In addition, consider that, even including these schools, only 29% of White people in the United States between the ages of 25 and 29 have a bachelor's degree at all.

Using the lens Alberti provides, I draw upon a yearlong ethnographic study of race and racism at James' and Laura's high school to examine White students' experiences with literacy and their postgraduation plans. James' and Laura's high school, Laurel Canyons, is located in a suburb but serves both rural and suburban students. It is moderately high achieving, with slightly higher than average scores on state standardized tests. The median home values in the district are above the state average, and fewer than 7% of the students qualify as "low-income." The school serves an overwhelmingly White student population, most of whom come from middle-class homes, judging by the population of adults in the district who have college degrees (nearly 40%) and the property values. Yet most of Laurel Canyons' students have modest college plans, and many of them do not plan to attend a four-year college at all. Of those who do, national statistics suggest that many won't finish (the overall percentage of the state's population that has a bachelor's degree was16% at the time of this research). Thus, these are students who only tentatively possess, or in some cases choose to forego, one of the fundamental material privileges associated with Whiteness: higher education.

By analyzing one Laurel Canyons student's story, I want to complicate the economic metaphors of White privilege in general and of White "ownership" of education and literacy in particular, and I argue for a view of Whiteness and of literacy as dynamic processes rather than static properties. The students I describe in this chapter do not support the widely held belief that middle-class White students have straightforward access to higher education and the economic and cultural privileges that it confers. This belief derives from a familiar dichotomy that pits privilege, literacy, enfranchisement, and Whiteness on one side, and non-White, working-class disenfranchisement, and illiteracy on the other. The students I describe here exist in socioeconomic borderlands beyond these categories. By taking a close look at the students' experiences in school, and by examining the "wages" their Whiteness supposedly confers in terms of literacy and access to higher education, I hope to move beyond such dichotomies.

This up-close view allows the dynamic and shifting relationships between literacy, access, and race to come into focus, suggesting that literacy, though it may be White property, as Prendergast suggests, is contested property, with a market value that is difficult to pin down. Ownership of it is a dynamic process involving rhetorical, curricular, and institutional struggle. Recognizing these—that "privilege," "access," even "literacy" itself are dynamic processes rather than static properties owned by Whites—leads to some revisions of current antiracist theory and research, as well as to a rethinking of pedagogies of Whiteness. Disentangling the associations between race and access will help antiracist educators recognize and address some of the limitations of classroom interrogations of Whiteness. Sherry Marx (2003) has recently noted that though these pedagogies aim to help White students understand White privilege, a growing body of classroom research, as well as much anecdotal evidence, suggests that, as Marx puts it, "enlightening discussions of racism in the classroom do not translate into antiracism once outside the classroom" (p. 4). The failures of pedagogies of Whiteness may stem in part from the ways economic metaphors for Whiteness (including the widely used metaphor of the "knapsack" of White privileges, a point I'll return to in the conclusion of this chapter) do not adequately capture the struggles for ownership of literacy, and the unsteady value of both racial identity and literacy, as they play out in school and in students' lived experiences.

Embedded in my argument that "privilege" is a process rather than a property are several key assumptions derived from recent work by Whiteness researchers Amanda Lewis (2003) and Pamela Perry (2002). As illustrated in chapter 3, Lewis focuses on the schools' role in ascribing racial identity to students. She argues that efforts to understand how racial identities influence educational outcomes often overlook the ways schools create racial meanings and promote particular racial identities. Schools, Lewis argues, teach the rules of racial classification and provide a space where students can practice them, and hence they are "race-making" institutions. Schools are not only places where White privilege operates to produce unequal outcomes (this is the view implied by the Whiteness-as-property metaphor); they are places where individuals and groups create, learn, and negotiate racial meanings, places where the property of Whiteness fluctuates in value depending on institutional and social contexts. Perry's study of two high schools makes a similar claim and suggests that rules of racial classification are intensely local, involving wide variation within broad racial descriptors: there are different ways of being "White" in different local contexts, and the meaning and value of Whiteness shifts across these contexts, making terms such as "privilege" difficult to pin down. At heart in both their studies is a desire to understand how White students develop their racial subjectivities in school and a sense that such understanding is central to future possibilities for racial equity in the United States. If, as they argue, schools play a role in the production of race as a social category both through implicit and explicit lessons and through school practices, then struggles over literacy, as I show in this chapter, are part of the apparatus of that production, part of a process by which racial ascriptions are made and racial meanings and values assigned.

I want to emphasize here that while I am advocating for more complexity in our metaphors for White privilege, I do not want to lose sight of the fundamental realities of racial inequality and race privilege in and out of school. In the story I am about to tell, for example, and in the emphasis I am about to place on the shifting and contradictory nature of White privilege, I want to be clear that privilege was nonetheless at work in the high school I studied, in the choices available to the students and parents, and in the educational and social power they are able to purchase for themselves (albeit at sometimes serious economic cost). This power as several studies have amply documented (see Kozol (2005) and Cashin (2004), for two of many examples), is not accessible, or not accessible to the same degree, to students of color and their families. That is, I do not want to lose sight of the very real system of Whiteness in place in public education and elsewhere. However, I do want to suggest here that the *metaphor* of Whiteness as property does not adequately capture the complexity of that system, and that we need to interrogate this metaphor, which, as

I suggest, can obscure the ways privilege is purchased, negotiated, sometimes rejected, and experienced.

Multicultural Literacy Education and White Racism

The research from which my argument is drawn addressed questions of multi-cultural literacy education and White racism through the stories of several high school seniors and their teacher as they read and wrote about race and identity over the course of the school year. In these stories, I focused on the meanings of White racial identity and attitudes toward race as these were constructed via schooling, in the terms and rhetorical structures of multicultural curricula, and in the cultural practices of literacy. I examined the rhetorical features of stu-dents' responses to multicultural texts—the "narrative gearshifts" (Morrison, 1992), metaphors, and discursive gestures that structure talk and writing about race; and I explored the vectors of influence—textual, pedagogical, social, and institutional—that shaped and gave rise to these constructions. This chapter draws from the last few months of the study, as students made postgraduation plans. I focus on one White student's experiences with a high-stakes literacy requirement and on her plans for the future, and I present these experiences in what Deborah Hicks calls "mixed" ethnographic genres in which narrative and reflection blur into one another.

The research site—Laurel Canyons High School—was 98.7% White, and as was the case in Lewis's (2003) study, not particularly unusual in this regard. Most White students in the United States attend schools like Laurel Canyons, schools that are almost entirely White. Most live in highly racially segregated neighborhoods and have little regular, substantial contact with people of other races. Yet this stark racial segregation tends to obscure other kinds of diversity; a closer look at Laurel Canyons reveals contradictory demographic details. One student's mother lacked a college degree and worked as a beautician, but his father had a college degree and worked in management; another student's father worked construction, but her mother was a schoolteacher. Yet another parent lived in a large house in one of the wealthier subdivisions but worked two jobs, at a drive-through window and at a clothing store in the mall.

The school itself reflected this socioeconomic ambiguity. The buildings and physical grounds of the school were typical of affluent suburban districts: the school was built eight years ago with state-of-the art athletic facilities, a theatre, art studio, large library with computers, and a number of periodicals. The classrooms were well appointed with books, computers, and artwork. The school's Web site boasts that 77% of its graduating seniors seek postsecondary education and 72% take the SAT, although for most students, postsecondary meant junior college, local business administration or technical colleges, or local state schools. Eighteen percent of the students were at the time of this study enrolled in special education programs, and the high school's state standardized test pass rate was just less than 70%. Only 6% of the school's students took the AP test, compared to 15% in similar schools, and the school had a drop-out rate of 2%.

When I asked students at Laurel Canyons to talk about why they chose their postgraduation plans, they spoke of the difficulty of amassing simultaneously different kinds of capital: economic, sociocultural, and academic. Some students had the grades and the money to go to college but chose a technical school because they didn't want to burden a working parent with sole care for a younger sibling. Some had parents who could afford to pay for college but didn't have the grades or couldn't complete the graduation requirements, or felt that college would take them too far from home; others lacked the financial resources but had taken AP classes and had straight A's and the solid encouragement of their teachers. Some couldn't imagine leaving behind friends. Others had parents, themselves with university degrees, who didn't believe college was worth the money, and felt that their own college degree hadn't proved to be worth much. The students' experiences demonstrate the difficulty of defining Whiteness in terms of class privilege or working-class disenfranchisement, and it highlights the complexity of access to education, which emerges in the students' experiences not as something owned by Whites but rather as a shifting site of varying value and availability.

Michelle's story illustrates these points. Michelle was a high school senior who lived with her mother (her parents were divorced) in a rented condominium in an affluent, gated subdivision near the school. She was enrolled in a required humanities course, the purpose of which was to help students with their Senior Projects, a high-stakes literacy requirement that entailed an oral presentation, a community service activity, and a formal academic research paper. A self-described "average" student who planned to attend a local junior college on graduation, Michelle was one of a number of students who had difficulty passing the research paper portion of the Senior Project, a requirement for graduation. Although the Senior Project was progressive in its intentions and design—it allowed for multiple literacy skills, asked students to participate meaningfully in a community project of their choice, and was widely viewed as a more authentic and student-centered assessment than the timed writing exams other districts used—the research paper portion of it was actually quite traditional. It asked students to develop a thesis, state it formally in the introduction, support it using library research, and document sources using MLA citation conventions.

In Michelle's eyes, the Senior Project was an unnecessary gatekeeper, the school's way of boosting its reputation at the expense of its students' needs: "The whole Senior Project thing? And like how you have to write a research paper? They're just trying to keep up with Lincoln [a neighboring school] and be like, our kids are so smart, and our scores are so high," she told me during class one day. Several parents, including Michelle's, echoed this view and felt like the school had "gone overboard" with the requirement, which was seen as too difficult for high school students, many of whom were not planning on attending college and would therefore, presumably, have no need for such research skills. As Michelle's teacher, Elizabeth, perceived it, parents wielded considerable power in the school, and their complaints about the Senior Project made it harder for her to do her job. She often talked about parents who "greased the wheels" for their children in ways that undermined the education she was trying to provide: parents who manipulated teachers into passing students who didn't meet requirements, or sought learning disability labels for their children to secure extra time and more lenient standards on projects. In addition, she was sometimes cautious in her curricular decisions and in assigning grades: "You have to be careful, because if you get one complaint, one parent phone call can change school policy." More immediately, for Elizabeth, a parent complaint could lead to administrative and school board review of her teaching, which in turn could mean even less freedom in the classroom than she already had.

Brantlinger (2003) describes this phenomenon as a "parentocracy," a term that refers to the control that White and middle-class parents have over schools and teachers. As she writes, parentocracies emerge when middle-class parents believe that advocating for school advantage for their children is integral to being a good parent. These parents often "unite in collective action to secure advantages for children of their class" (p. 11). Typically, a parentocracy works to ensure that certain children are placed in the highest tracks with the "best" teachers. However, at Laurel Canyons, parents also worked to get their children diagnosed with learning disabilities, because the label came with extra time on tests and ensured that less-rigorous standards would be used in evaluating the student's work, thus making it easier for the student to graduate with a high–grade point average. In addition, as we see in the following text, parents sometimes advocated making the curriculum less rigorous, or "elitist," in parents' words, often out of fear that high standards would work against their child's success.

When Michelle, along with several other students, received a "No Credit" on the rough draft of the research paper for failing to use any library sources or otherwise not conforming to the strict guidelines laid out in the assignment, a handful of parents began to advocate against the Senior Project, arguing that it was discriminatory. In a long letter sent to Elizabeth and the school administration, one of these parents employed a kind of working-class rhetoric against the school and its literacy requirements as gatekeepers to middle-class prosperity. At the same time, she expressed resistance to the particular kind of White middle-classness the school implicitly promoted via its literacy requirements: "Graduation should be about fun memories and walking across the stage with friends," this parent wrote, "not worrying about whether you wrote a paper with proper footnotes.... Not all students are meant to be a mathematician or journalist or doctor. What about the average child?" She went on to discuss her sense that the school's curriculum discriminated against "average" students, and argued that the literacy requirements most students would need in workplace did not include knowledge of MLA citation conventions or library research skills.

Many parents at Laurel Canyons shared this view and thus they approached the Senior Project in ways that undermined its intent—helping students get around various aspects of its requirements, in some cases even helping students forge aspects of it. Nationwide, as the *Wall Street Journal* recently reported, many parents resent the time burdens that Senior Projects, increasingly used as a high-stakes requirement tied to graduation, place on their families, and were convinced that Senior Projects turn teachers into "nit-picking, power-wielding maniacs," determining students' futures by counting page numbers, combing through MLA citations looking for errors, or failing students' oral presentations on the smallest of details.

But parents, one administrator told me, "just don't understand what the school is trying to do." In his view:

> At Lincoln, and North High, they have super high SATs. But we've got kids who do everything right and then don't even apply [to college]. You tell them to take AP classes, take the SAT, apply to college, and their parents are like, college is too

expensive, they're going to [the local junior college], and these are well-off parents! The same parents who complain the second anything goes wrong around here. The rural families would kill for those opportunities, and we can't get our high-achieving kids to have high aspirations. We have a five year plan to raise aspirations, to start younger with the kids, get them psyched for college. It's straightforward with the rural community: you make sure they know the options, have access to financial aid, make sure their kids take the right classes, and we've done that here. We have open tracks, kids self-select, and you can see kids right off the farm in AP history and AP English and doing well. But you take these Crimson kids [kids from the well-off suburbs and townships that feed into the school], and they have everything, and they do well, and their parents are super involved in the school, and you get to the moment of college choice, and they'll take [the state school] or [community college], anything to save a buck, keep their kids close to them. They have this idea that it's all just foolish and a waste of time. It's like one of them said, 'my kid doesn't need a fancy diploma from a fancy school. Just make sure he graduates and I'll take care of the rest.' Mediocrity is our problem. A lot of parents can't imagine sending their kids off to college, can't afford it, maybe, but just don't want to imagine it…

The contradictory reversals at work here—where working-class Whites take advantage of progressive school policies to send their children to college while more privileged middle-class Whites refuse to do so, and instead use parentocratic tools to ensure "mediocrity" for their children—make clear that the notion of White ownership of literacy does not fully capture the complex relationship between privilege and schooling at Laurel Canyons. Literacy may be White property, as Prendergast (2003) suggests, but at Laurel Canyons, it is contested property, with a market value that is difficult to pin down. Struggles over who owns it—manifest in struggles over the Senior Project and in students' postgraduation plans—suggest that as much as Whites may ratchet up the value of literacy to keep their own status and mark racial boundaries, they also exert a downward pressure on it, as they work to keep literacy affordable for themselves. As the value of literacy goes up, as literacy becomes more and more high priced, Whites at Laurel Canyons struggled against this inflation to ensure their share.

Beyond the Invisible Knapsack: Rethinking Metaphors for Whiteness in the Classroom

I'd like to turn now to some reflections on the scholarship addressing antiracist education. This is a site where the complexity of the relationship between

Whiteness and privilege is most obscured, and where the need for exploration of that complexity is most severe. The growing body of scholarship on
"critical pedagogies of Whiteness" (Applebaum, 2003) points to the myriad
ways that such pedagogies fall short. Kathy Hytten and John Warren (2003),
Audrey Thompson (2003), and Lewis, Ketter, and Fabos (2001), for example,
all write of White students who refuse to discuss racial injustice or otherwise
resist antiracism. Alice McIntyre (1997) describes how difficult it is for even
well-intentioned White teachers to engage in critiques of White privilege.

Much of this research posits a characterization of White students as privileged—benefiting from an unjust racial hierarchy in the United States—and
therefore as unwilling to engage with texts or ideas that analyze privilege and
suggest the need for social change.

This research often draws from one of the most powerful iterations of the
Whiteness-as-property metaphors, McIntosh's (1992) seminal "White Privilege:
Unpacking the Knapsack." In this essay, McIntosh describes White privilege as
an "invisible package of unearned assets that [Whites] can count on cashing in
each day, but about which [Whites are] meant to remain oblivious" (p. 291).
This formulation suggests that privilege is a tangible commodity one owns and
can use like currency, trading it for other tangible commodities. Applebaum's
(2003) discussion of her experiences teaching McIntosh's essay suggests the
difficulty White students have in understanding White privilege:

> A number of months ago, after what I considered to be a good discussion of Peggy
> McIntosh's influential article, I asked my students to identify three examples of how
> privilege, in the sense that McIntosh articulates, works on our own campus. Among
> the response I received to my requests for dominant group privileges that can be seen
> today on our campus, however, were:
>
> Females get free drinks at the bars while males have to pay all the time.
>
> Females get taken out on dates and the men pay for them.
>
> Students who work in the dining hall get free food.
>
> Being part of this university will get your foot in the door when you apply for a job.
>
> Tall people have privilege in college basketball.
>
> Blacks and other minorities have privilege because they get athletic scholarships and
> affirmative action benefits. (p. 8)

Analyzing these responses, Applebaum points out the resistance embedded
in her White students' seemingly willful misunderstanding of the concept of

dominant group privilege: "Not only do some of my students fail to appreciate the systemic nature of dominant group privilege ... they also do not see how the oppression of people of color systemically sustains and makes possible dominant group privilege" (p. 8).

I'd like to suggest a slightly different interpretation of Applebaum's students' responses. I'd like to suggest that her students do not appreciate the systemic nature of privilege because they don't experience privilege systemically. What they experience are "contradictions in subjective experiences and in educational discourses" (Levine-Rasky, 2000, p. 274) of the sort I have chronicled at Laurel Canyons. What they experience is a system of privileges that is in flux, and whose values are not guaranteed. In this way, to characterize Whiteness as a wage that confers systemic privileges, that indicates a particular economic relationship to literacy, and to see Whiteness as a wage that can purchase literacy and Whites as thus owning it, is to miss much about the contested nature of literacy, race, and class.

Michelle had planned to attend a local community college with her best friend, Lisa, but that spring her enthusiasm for this plan dimmed considerably. Lisa had decided to go to a four-year college, several miles to the south, because her parents felt like she should do something with her life, and get away from the "trashy elements" at the junior college. "You know, it's just a lot of the same kids from here, and from Carville [a nearby working-class township] and it's very low-life," Lisa said in class one day, with a typical lack of tact.

Michelle snorted. "She means me." She turned to me, "Her mom thinks like I'm a bad influence ...That's why they won't let her go to [the junior college]. They want her to get away from me."

"It's kind of true," Lisa conceded. "They think if I go there I'll just hang out with the same high school crowd and it will bring me down."

Throughout the school year, in an effort to understand how the students thought about race, I conducted interviews with students and asked them to describe their first memories of learning about race and racism. Michelle's story stood out because of its focus on school and its complicating narrative articulation of the relationship between race, schooling, and privilege; in her story, we can see how White perceptions and experiences of privilege, particularly in terms of school, are not readily explained by economic metaphors of school as White property.

> I had this friend in junior high. I didn't go here. We lived in Sharpsville where my
> mom is from then, and I went to Junior High there, and we moved because it's kind

of a rough school, you know? Not as good as here. But, in seventh grade, me and this girl, Sheila, were best friends, and she was Black. It didn't mean anything to me. We had like all our classes together, and if it was alphabetical we sat by each other because her name was right after mine. I didn't have a lot of friends there, because there are so many losers who live in that district, which is why we moved. But Sheila was cool. And we hung out all the time. She was really funny, and would always crack me up. And we got in trouble in class a lot, we would like goof around, mouth off to teachers, and they were always like calling my parents and stuff. And one day, we got in trouble...and the teacher sent us to different rooms so we would stop talking and goofing around, and to me she was like, why do you hang out with her? She's getting you in trouble. She was all, Michelle you're college material, you're going somewhere, and she's not, and she's bringing you down. I can see it happening. And I was all, whatever. It still pisses me off. I guess she thought, like because my dad has money, and like went to college, that I was all "college material," but you know what? I'm totally not. And my parents, they're fine with it. My sister went, but I'm all, I don't want to leave my friends, and my grades suck, and I'm just totally not college material. And my dad's like, that's fine. I think he doesn't want me to leave my mom, because then he'd have to deal with her. And my mom thinks college is expensive for what it is, you know? You can get the same thing at [the local community college], or even better, they have really good teachers there, and it costs like half the price for tuition. My mom just wants me to learn something useful so I can get a job, and she's always all, Michelle, what are they teaching you at that school? It's ridiculous, half the stuff we read in here, it's not going to help in the workforce, and my mom knows it. I think college is kind of overrated, if you ask me.

There is no doubt that in fundamental respects this is a story of White privilege and the education that Whiteness can purchase. Michelle's Whiteness garners a favorable impression of her from her teacher, which results in the kinds of encouragement that students need if they are going to succeed. Moreover, Michelle's parents, at least in part because they are White, possessed the resources to move out of a school district that was too "rough," thus ensuring a "better" education for their daughter. These are the kinds of privileges that are generally invisible to most Whites, as McIntosh illustrates.

But at the same time, the issues Michelle's story raises—racism, educational access, the uses and usefulness of literacy, privilege—complicate the economic metaphors of Whiteness as a "wage," "investment," "property," or perk one can pull out of a knapsack. Privilege, in Michelle's narrative is not a static quantity that, as a White person, she owns and uses. Rather, it emerges in her narrative as a complex process that mutates and shifts across contexts. For Michelle, the "privilege" of literacy and access that her Whiteness gives her is a commodity of unstable value, and she grasps it fleetingly. Positioned as possessing access to education—"you're college material" her teacher tells her—she is also alienated from it by her friendship with a person of color, and perhaps more complexly, by own sense that education is more limiting than advantageous, an expensive waste that will take her away from friends and family and provide her with skills she and her family believe she won't need.

None of this is to say that Michelle's access to literacy is less direct or less straightforward than, for example, her friend Sheila's. In this case, the teacher's personal racist assumptions have invidious consequences for both girls. Similarly, Michelle's family's decision to move (and ability to do so) is permeated by economic and institutional racism. But it is to say that teachers must be willing to help White students understand systemic racial inequality, and investigate with them the specific, complex, and contradictory ways in which Whites "own" literacy and other privileges. We must be willing to reach out to White students by examining the dynamic and processual nature of that ownership.

Complicating this will be the difficulty of pinning down in any meaningful way the value and significance of what it means to be White at all. To say that Michelle is "White" without also signifying her socioeconomic class identity makes the racial designation almost meaningless (consider the connotative difference between "Working-class White" and "middle-class White" in terms of what we assume about privilege). But assigning a class identity to Michelle is difficult, as I've tried to suggest throughout this chapter. Lewis' notion of ascription is relevant here. Embedded in Michelle's story are assumptions that help teach Michelle what it means to be White, assumptions that in their enactment help Michelle acquire the "rules of racial classification"—an understanding of White identity and its relationship to other identities. Michelle and her family can't be adequately described as either middle or working class. They are not part of a powerful and affluent parentocracy advocating advantage for themselves via schooling. Nor can we describe them as disempowered members of the working class, with all the educational inequality, discrimination, and alienation that such working-class status entails. Yet, through the processes of schooling, Michelle acquires a racial identity that positions her in particular ways vis-a-vis her education and vis-a-vis literacy.

In the end, only a handful of the students I got to know in the course of my research at Laurel Canyons ended up going to four-year universities. Laura, the student we met in the introduction, was one of them. She planned to go to State in the fall. She had decided to live at home though, to save money, and because, as she said, her own home was "a lot nicer than the dorms." James decided to forego school and work in his cousin's garage. Michelle went to the local junior college, where she hoped to use the Associate's degree to get a job as an administrative assistant, like her mother.

Understanding the vast socioeconomic terrain these students inhabit—somewhere in-between working and middle class—seems crucial to understanding the meanings of their Whiteness, its privileges, and its relationship to literacy and its institutions. To get there may require relinquishing the socioeconomic and racial categories of analysis that literacy researchers have relied upon. In her race-inflected reading of Shirley Brice Heath's (1983) *Ways with Words*, for example, Prendergast (2003) examines how ethnography produces "typifications" (Abu-Lod) that inadvertently forward the notion of literacy as White property. In her analysis of the "absent presence" of race in Heath's research, Prendergast analyzes Heath's field notes and documents from her Piedmont literacy study, and discovers how ethnography, like schooling, maintains White privilege even when it is ostensibly aimed at deconstructing it. Toward this end, it is worth remembering that Heath's pivotal study rests on the ethnographic construction of three communities, one Black, one working-class White, and one middle-class White. The working-class community, as Prendergast points out, is described in ways that make it appear as different from the middle-class community as the Black community appears to be. However, as Prendergast suggests,

> The history of desegregation in the area suggests that White mainstreamers and the White working class had an imagined community of their own—an identification based on race that crossed class lines. Schools were seen as mechanisms through which those racial lines might be maintained, even as economic disparities became starker. (p. 85)

As my research ended, I came back again and again to the school's Web site and its claim that 79% of its students seek postsecondary education. When I first read that claim, I imagined, as perhaps the Web site's creators had hoped I would, most of the graduating class heading off to universities and liberal arts colleges, the luckier among them to Harvard and Yale. In this way the claim of 77% works to create an imagined community of middle-class Whites, an imagined community that is supported by multicultural pedagogies that make few, if any, class distinctions in their descriptions of racial groups. Perhaps even more disconcertingly, multicultural pedagogies also fail to address in any meaningful way the needs and desires of students like Michelle. Addressing such students will require getting beyond metaphors that equate White racial identity with tangible assets and toward seeing Whiteness as a series of ongoing strategies and negotiations—as a process. What would it mean to bring this perspective, rather than McIntyre's "knapsack," into the antiracist classroom for students like Michelle? To teach White students about the power of their imagined community, and to compare that power with their own experiences of privilege, with their struggles to attain it, and their skepticism toward it? These are questions that must be addressed if we are to teach successfully against racism, and if we are to disentangle the complex—albeit persistent—relationship between Whiteness and privilege.

Note

1. All names, including those of places and institutions, are pseudonyms.

References

Alberti, J. (2001). Returning to class; Creating opportunities for multicultural reform at majority second-tier schools. *College English, 63*, 561–584.

Applebaum, B. (2003). White privilege, complicity, and the social construction of race. *Educational Foundations*, 5–20.

Brantlinger, E. (2003). *Dividing classes: How the middle class negotiates and rationalizes school advantage.* New York: Routledge.

Cashin, S. (2004). *The failures of integration: How race and class are undermining the American dream.* New York: Public Affairs.

Harris, C. (1991). Whiteness as property. *Harvard Law Review, 106*, 1707–1791.

Heath, S. B. (1983). *Ways with words.* Cambridge: Cambridge University Press.

Hytten, K., & Warren, J. (2003). Engaging whiteness: How racial power gets reified in education. *Qualitative Studies in Education, 16*(1), 65–89.

Ladson-Billings, G., & Tate, W. (1995). Toward a critical race theory of education. *Teachers College Record, 97*(1), 47–68.

Levine-Rasky, C. (2000). Framing whiteness: Working through the tensions in introducing whiteness to educators. *Race, Ethnicity and Education, 3*(3), 271–292.

Lewis, A. (2003). *Race in the schoolyard: Negotiating the color line in classrooms and communities.* New Brunswick, NJ: Rutgers University Press.

Lewis, C., Ketter, J., & Fabos, B. (2001). Reading race in a rural contest. *Qualitative Studies in Education, 13*, 317–350.

Lipsitz, G. (1998). *The possessive investment in whiteness: How white people profit from identity politics.* Philadelphia: Temple University Press.

Marx, S. (2003). Reflections on the state of critical white studies. *International Journal of Qualitative Studies in Education, 16*(1), 3–5.

McIntosh, P. (1992). White privilege and male privilege: A personal account of coming to see correspondences through work in women's studies. In M. L. Anderson & P. H. Collins (Eds.), *Race, class, and gender: An anthology* (pp. 70–81). Belmont, CA: Wadsworth.

McIntyre, A. (1997). *Making meaning of whiteness: Exploring racial identity with white teachers.* New York: SUNY Press.

Morrison, T. (1992). *Playing in the dark: Whiteness and the literary imagination.* New York: Vintage Books.

Perry, P. (2002). *Shades of white: White kids and racial identities in high school.* Durham, NC: Duke University Press.

Pope, D. (2001). *Doing school: How we are creating a generation of stressed out, materialistic, and miseducated students.* New Haven, CT: Yale University Press.

Prendergast, C. (2003). *Literacy and racial justice: The politics of learning after Brown v. Board of Education.* Carbondale, IL: Southern University Press.

Roediger, D. (1991). *The wages of whiteness: Race and the making of the American working class.* New York: Verso.

Thompson, A. (2003). Tiffany, friend of people of color: White investments in antiracism. *International Journal of Qualitative Studies in Education, 16*(1), 7–29.

· 6 ·

"TAMING THE BEAST":
RACE, DISCOURSE, AND IDENTITY
IN A MIDDLE SCHOOL CLASSROOM

ADRIENNE DIXSON

This chapter presents data from a research project conducted in three urban middle schools in a large Midwestern public school district. Whereas the primary focus of the research project was aimed at the perceptions and experiences of "urban" middle school students, this chapter takes a closer look at the sometimes competing interests and agendas of students and teachers. Specifically, I explore a theme that emerged as significant throughout the course of the study, that is students' and teachers' conceptualizations of the students' racial identities were not synchronous, but quite often contradictory. As a result, there was little, if any, progress made to the extent that "school" literacy events were both relevant and meaningful for students.

Using the Critical Race Theory (CRT) tenet of the critique of liberalism, I examine how the teachers' constructions of students at times served as a barrier to literacy pedagogies that could have drawn on and supported the cultural wealth (Yosso, 2006) that students brought into the classroom. These constructions of the students created a tension that stood in contrast to the students' sophisticated understandings of their own racialized identities particularly around literacy (Heath, 1983) and speech events

(Hymes, 1964). Consequently, the teachers premised their literacy approaches on the notion that students lack the ability to "decode" text; thus, they needed reading materials at significantly lower levels than that of their suburban peers. Moreover, literacy materials selected for use in the classrooms discussed in this chapter reflect the teachers' racialized conceptualization and ontological understanding of the students. The exchanges around literacy materials serve as gatekeeping mechanisms that deny "these urban students" greater participation in literacy and school success. As Prendergast (2003) has noted, historically, African Americans have faced numerous attempts by Whites to deny them access to mainstream literacy. This chapter examines the ways in which African American students continue to struggle for "literacy as a civil right."

Theoretical Framework

The history of CRT both in the legal field and in education has been well documented (Crenshaw, Gotanda, Peller, & Thomas, 1995; Dixson & Rousseau, 2005; Ladson-Billings & Tate, 1995; Tate, 1997). CRT scholars in education argue that CRT provides a lens through which to examine the ways in which educational practices, policies, and curricula help to maintain a system of White supremacy that not only frames what students can know and learn, but also casts African American students in a negative light in order to justify these same restrictive and oppressive practices (Chapman, 2006; DeCuir & Dixson, 2004; Dixson, 2006; Duncan, 2006; Ladson-Billings & Tate, 1995; Rousseau, 2006; Yosso, 2006). Although educators and policy makers may not be overtly racist, seemingly neutral educational policies designed for "all" students call attention to the limitations of a liberal, color-blind ideology. That is, under the auspices of equality rather than equity and color blindness rather than color-consciousness, most educational policies and practices have the unintentional (or intentional) consequence of disproportionately impacting African American students negatively. Given these limitations, I situate my analysis of the teachers' discourses within the CRT tenets of the critique of liberalism and color blindness to examine the ways in which their constructions of students both shaped and limited the students' access to classroom literacy events. I also draw upon the students' counternarratives to address the ways in which youth's understandings of themselves as learners are in many instances at odds with what their teachers believe.

Methodology

For this study, I drew upon a conceptualization of ethnography I describe as a jazz methodology (Dixson, 2005). I conceptualized this methodology on the notion that research is creative, interactive, and political. Drawing on what Ladson-Billings (2000) describes as "racialized epistemologies and ethnic discourses," this methodology is significantly informed by Lawrence-Lightfoot's (1994) portraiture and her notion of a "search for goodness," not pathology. As such, I framed the research that informs this chapter with the understanding that "urban" students, and primarily low-income African American students who attend urban schools, are "good." In contrast to much of the research focusing on urban middle schools, which often casts urban adolescents as deficient, violent, and disinterested in learning, I assume that urban students bring a wealth of knowledge to their schooling contexts. Further, I believe that the student's wealth of knowledge relates to their racial and cultural identities (Ladson-Billings, 1994; Lee, 2003; Lee, Spencer, & Harpalani, 2003; Lesko, 2001; Moll, 1992). Furthermore, my interest in this study was in the ways in which "healthy" students negotiate particular schooling contexts and pedagogical practices (Irvine, 1990; Ladson-Billings, 1994; Lee, 2003; Lesko, 2001).

Through this ethnographic study, I examined the following questions: (a) What are urban students' perceptions of middle school? (b) How do urban students' perceptions of middle school compare and contrast with their academic and social experiences? (c) How do students' and teachers' understanding of the students' racial identities affect the academic experiences that the students have in school (i.e., with literacy, numeracy, etc.). Using participant-observation, data were collected in classrooms, specials (art, music, computer), cafeteria, and hallways at Jamison Middle School, located in Camden, a growing metropolitan area in the Midwest with a large urban district.[1] I also conducted ethnographic interviews with students, parents, teachers, and administrators. For this study, I focused on the sixth-grade students and teachers in part to get a sense of how students' perceptions of middle school develop over time. The data were collected from October 2005 to June 2006. It is important to note that, when possible, I matched interviewers by race and gender. The exception was that the same White male graduate student interviewed all the White participants regardless of gender. Given that some of the interview questions were explicitly focused on race and racism, I decided to match interviewers and participants by race to ensure that respondents felt comfortable answering questions of that nature.

Site and Participants

Jamison, an Urban Institute (UI: a school the district designed to be an exemplary urban school) drew students from a variety of elementary schools in the Camden Public Schools. Although students came from a variety of elementary schools across the city, the feeder school was one of the two UI elementary schools. In 2005, the district's Director of the Urban Institutions, Mavis Roy, asked me to help her understand what she saw as significant issues at Jamison, in terms of student engagement and general behavioral concerns. The district had four UIs—two elementary schools, a middle school, and a high school. It appeared that, for the most part, the elementary schools were successful in terms of engaging students, given that school attendance was high and test scores in reading were in the passing range. In contrast, the Director lamented that, at the middle school, students who seemed to thrive at the elementary level experienced a significant decline such that by eighth grade many seemed to be completely disconnected and disengaged from school. To examine this issue related to engagement as well as to gain an understanding of what students thought about middle school, I designed the study to follow the students as they entered middle school. In terms of whom I would invite to participate in the study, I made no distinction between high- and low-achieving students. I initially invited students on the basis of whether or not they attended one of the two UIs in fifth grade. In total, I invited approximately one hundred fifth-grade students from both the UI elementary schools to participate in the study. Approximately one-quarter (27) of the students invited agreed to participate in the study.

Although the district assigned most of the UI elementary school students to either Jamison or Marysville Middle School, a number of students, particularly those assigned to Jamison, attended either another middle school in the district or a charter school. To ascertain whether engagement was an issue peculiar to Jamison or something that may be pervasive in middle schools in general, I included the other middle schools that a majority of the UI elementary school students attended. It is important to note that the district experiences a significant amount of transience. In addition, the growth of charter schools in the city has affected the district in terms of its student population and consequently its funding base. As a result, I had to open up the sample at Jamison to students who had not attended a UI school in large part because the students assigned to Jamison did not come to the school and did not provide forwarding information. The enrollment was so low at Jamison that the principal asked teachers to call students who had not reported to school to find out whether they were just missing school or whether they had transferred to another school. Consequently, owing to the school's decline in enrollment among other issues unrelated to the declining enrollment, the district closed Jamison at the end of the school year.

Not unlike many urban school districts, Camden Public Schools serve a large minority population. The district afforded opportunities to students of color and White students to attend lottery schools and special alternative schools located throughout the city. Ironically, students living in Peaceful Hamlet primarily attended schools outside of the area, either in private, specialized public or charter schools. Both Jamison and its feeder elementary school sit literally across the street from homes with school-age children who do not attend either school. DeGaulle's (see page 131) characterization of Jamison captures the general perception of the school: "When I first went to Jamison we had 10 sixth graders … Cause nobody says, 'oh, let's go there.' That's not exactly on their list. Even though it is a pretty good place once you get there. But because the building's old and raggedy looking it gets a bad rep" (DeGaulle Interview, 2005).

It is within this backdrop that Jamison students and teachers emerge as an interesting case not only because of the school's reputation in the district for violence[2] and lagging achievement, but also because the students' demeanor and interests belied its reputation. In addition, despite the fact that I had informed the teachers that my focus was on the students and not on their teaching, inevitably, the teachers would share their lesson plans for the day or ask me what I thought about the lessons and materials they had selected. Anna Green, one of the social studies and language arts teachers, most frequently requested this type of feedback from me. Thus, while I tried to focus solely on the students, the teachers' interactions with and overall demeanor toward the students became prominent.

The entire second floor of Jamison was dedicated to the sixth grade. The grade level consisted of two teams, each configured with two content area teachers (math/science and language arts/social studies) and a special education teacher. The second floor was the most well-lit floor in the building with the exception of the main floor on which the office was located. The first floor, where the seventh grade was housed, and the third floor, where the eighth grade was housed, had very few working lights in the hallway. The basement, where specials such as art, music, and computer technology were taught, as well as where the cafeteria was located, was the most poorly lit area of the school. The building, a nineteenth-century construction, closed at the end of the school year, and the students were assigned to various other schools in the district.

Anna Nicole Green

Green's room is located on the second floor of Jamison.

Green had been a sixth-grade language arts and social studies teacher at Jamison for five years. She spent 6 of her 11 years as a teacher at the elementary school that fed into Jamison before making the transition to teaching middle school students. She is White and in her mid-thirties. She maintained strict control over the physical movements of her students and they were to remain seated at all times, unless she gave them permission to move or change seats. Students who got out of their seats without permission, talked out of turn, or talked too loudly would either get a warning and/or would have to serve a lunch detention. In chronic cases of this type of misbehavior, Green would send students out of the classroom to the office or write a disciplinary referral (an I-90) that went to the Assistant Principal, Rowley. For most students, the simple threat of having to serve a lunch detention was a significant deterrent for bad behavior. To encourage good behavior, Green distributed tickets to students for various types of behaviors. At times she awarded tickets to students for doing specific things: following directions, turned in homework on time, or sitting quietly in their seats at dismissal. At other times, she awarded tickets for no particular reason. Students would receive a treat at the end of the week based on the number of tickets they had accumulated. The treats ranged from candy bars to books to a $5 compact disc player that she had purchased from Wal-Mart. In essence, Green's classroom was her domain and not the students'.

She organized the classroom such that students sat in groups of 4–6 at one of the seven small round tables. The seating arrangement seemed to contradict the collaborative spirit that round tables, rather than desks in rows, generally engender, as along with the restriction she placed on students' physical movement, Green also prohibited students from talking to each other. On each table were "paper folder holders"—cardboard magazine holders—that sat in front of the students. Officially, and according to Green, she used the folder holders to help students stay organized because she believed that middle school students, especially sixth-grade students, struggle with organization. Unofficially, the students used the folder holders for subversive purposes that facilitated communication among each other without Green noticing. Despite the fact that students sat at tables rather than desks, the general classroom organization did not facilitate a flow of traffic for students or adults. Learning was generally focused on the front of the classroom where the chalkboard, overhead screen, and Green were located.

Green decorated the classroom with a variety of commonly found commercial materials ranging from posters on the writing process, "values" and citizenship rules, as well as "famous" people of color like Rosa Parks. In addition to the commercial decorations, in the classroom was also, literally, a broken record. That is, prominently displayed on one wall was a timeline of Black History on a teacher-created, paper record album that was missing three pieces. Green described the record as having a "Motown feel" and explained that she used the record to connect with her African American students. However, she had lost three pieces of the album, so it literally looked like a broken record. Green explained that she had lost the three pieces in her move from her previous school, although she had been at Jamison for five years. After observing her classroom for 10 months, Green had not replaced the three missing pieces. I could not help but conclude that the timeline inadvertently, or, perhaps, dysconsciously (King, 1991) contradicted her feeling that she tried to reach out to her students and connect with their sense of history and culture.

Ellen DeGaulle

Ellen DeGaulle was a 20-year veteran teacher at Jamison Middle School. She is a White female in her mid-to-late forties. DeGaulle had taught in Camden for 12 years. Before coming to Camden, she taught in both a rural school district in Ohio and a large urban school district on the East Coast. Before coming to the middle school, she also taught at the African-centered high school located about one mile away from Jamison.

She had taught language arts on the other sixth-grade team but the principal reassigned her to the seventh grade after the school's 30-day count revealed that enrollment was significantly low. She was moved from the second floor to a new classroom located on the poorly lit third floor. The physical arrangement of the third floor was in many ways a stark contrast to the second floor. The location and physical arrangement of the lockers on the third floor created an obstacle that made physical maneuverability awkward for both teachers and students. They often blocked the entry of classrooms and served as barriers for teachers to interact with students or to view students' interactions with each other. The high ceilings created acoustic challenges, and students' and teachers' voices reverberated throughout the hallway and downstairs to the second floor. The din often created a disturbance during instructional time. As the class schedules for the sixth-, seventh-, and eighth-grade students were different, anything that required the seventh graders to travel downstairs disrupted both the sixth- and eighth-grade classrooms. The seventh-grade students had the reputation of being out of control. Most teachers and administrators described them as "aliens" because they often returned to school very different, not only in terms of physical attributes, but also in terms of their behavior and demeanor, from how they were when they were in the sixth grade.

DeGaulle was a conscientious teacher who took advantage of the wide array of professional development workshops that the district offered. During both formal interviews and informal conversations, she referenced a workshop she had attended and described how she was implementing the newest strategy she had learned. After having attended a workshop on differentiation and reading instruction, DeGaulle learned that having books on tape might help students who were struggling with reading. Although the workshop facilitators suggested that books on tape was a strategy that represented good teaching for special education students, DeGaulle saw it as a strategy that she would use with all of her students despite their reading ability. Almost without exception, she exclusively used books on tapes with her students. The only books her students read in class were the ones that she could find on tape. The entire class read the same book; students rarely, if ever, read independently. DeGaulle applied this strategy to her seventh-grade students as well.

Denzel Williams

Denzel Williams was a 12-year-old African American male on Green's team. (Grade levels are organized into teams. There are two sixth-grade teams. One consists of a language arts/social studies teacher, a math/science teacher, and a special education teacher. The other team is math/science, social studies, language arts, and a special education teacher who floats among all three classrooms). At the time of this study, he had lived in and attended the Camden Public Schools for five years. He was originally from Tylertown, a medium-sized city located west of Camden. Denzel was "cute" and captured the attention of a number of his female classmates. Dressed generally in the "gear" of his peer group—baggy jeans, oversized white t-shirts, and his hair in cornrows—Denzel was not oblivious to the fact that he had a number of admirers. His style of dress belied the fact that he was a conscientious student and generally completed all of his assigned work. An affable young man with a sarcastic sense of humor, he was one of the few students, boys in particular, who managed to avoid lunch detentions because of missing class or homework. During my visits to the classroom, I found him to be quiet and generally focused on completing his work. I noted that on the days that he was the focal student, it took some time for him to warm up to me. Like most of the students who participated in the study, he was usually interested in reading my field notes especially when he was the focal student. My practice had been to sit in the seat next to the day's focal student. As such, I openly shared the notes I took while observing him and explained why I was taking note of particular events. He would often make fun of my handwriting because he found it illegible. Despite being friendly, funny, and open with me, when I gave him the option of having either me conduct his interview or my graduate assistant, Andre—an African American male who had dreadlocks—he preferred to have Andre conduct the interview. In addition, he would frequently ask about Andre, or "the dark dude with the dreadlocks" and whether he would be visiting the class to "take notes on him" too.

His mother, Sherry, was critical of the school district. With Jamison's impending closing, she entered Denzel in the district's lottery to attend one of the alternative middle schools rather than the one that the district selected to house the misplaced Jamison students. Both she and Denzel hoped he would get into the district's only African-centered school that went from kindergarten through twelfth grade.

Makayla James

Makayla was a 12-year-old African American female on Guinevere's team. She was born and raised in Camden and the younger of two girls. Her older sister was a freshman in high school.

A thoughtful yet complex young woman, Makayla often found very creative ways to get excused from her academic classes to go home or would skip them and roam the school building. Despite her disinterest in her classes, she was insightful, bright, and generally respectful to most adults and students. She would, however, "cuss" someone out, be it teacher, principal, or student if she felt she had been disrespected. She believed in respecting her "elders," but believed that they also had to be respectful to her. She had a wonderful sense of humor, and my interactions with her were always pleasant.

Teachers' and Students' Understanding of Students' Racial Identities

Although I designed the study to understand students' perceptions of and experiences in middle school, the data suggest that students' and teachers' conceptualizations of the students' racial identities operated in contradiction to each other. In addition, in light of this contradiction, "school" literacy experiences tended to lack relevancy and meaning for students. The data illuminate two subthemes in this area:

1. The teachers, primarily White females, had little understanding of the students' racial identities, and they generally framed the students, the students' capabilities and the students' literacy abilities within discourses of deficiency related to race that "othered" and encoded troubling stereotypes of "these urban students," their families, and the communities in which the students lived;

2. Conversely, the students had a highly sophisticated understanding of their racialized identities; however, the teachers silenced the students, either through overt or through tacit strategies. In particular, literacy (Heath, 1983) and speech events (Hymes, 1964) could have been more meaningful and relevant for students given their understanding of their own racial identities if teachers valued and drew upon their cultural wealth (Yosso, 2006).

The teacher-student interactions in these classrooms reified an asymmetrical power relationship through which the teacher-directed literacy approach (positioned as the dominant discourse and dominant operating practice) was premised on the notion that the students lack the ability to "decode" text and, therefore, needed reading materials at significantly lower levels than what they were actually capable of and interested in reading. The data also suggest that the students have sophisticated literacy and language abilities that the teachers did not recognize owing in large part to the ways in which the teachers framed and understood students.

"Taming the Beast"

When asked which teacher he would recommend to the next year's sixth graders, Denzel stated he would recommend the only African American teacher on
the team, Armstrong. In contrast, he gave Green's name as one he hoped that
students would not have as a teacher. He described her in the following way:

> She jump up on the chair a lot and yell and everything. That's why I get spooked, she
> jump up on the chair and then she start yelling at everybody. Me and Sherman, we
> stop and look and we just get back to our work cause there's no telling her, 'cause if
> you tell her she'll just say "well I don't care.

Denzel views Green and her behavior in class as volatile and dismissive of
students' requests. Denzel's description of Green is an interesting contrast to
the popular descriptions of urban students as volatile, disinterested in learning, and loud.

Similarly, Teena Marie, the only White student in Green's class, describes
her as "mean" when asked to describe her teachers:

Interviewer (I)	:	What do you see when you look at your teachers?
Teena Marie (TM)	:	Mean
I	:	Mean?
TM	:	Yep.
I	:	Give me an example.
TM	:	I look at Ms. Green like she's gonna start yelling.
I	:	Does she yell at you a lot?
TM	:	She yells at EVERYBODY a lot.

Green believes that she is keenly aware of what her students need. In the
exchange below, she describes the characteristics of a teacher who is suitable
for teaching middle school students, framing her description on the popular
construction of the erratic and hormone-driven adolescent (Lesko, 2001).

Green: …"I think sometimes they place the wrong people in the buildings.
I think there are teachers here and elsewhere that have high school certifi-
cations and they can't get into high schools so they go to middle school and
they treat this like it's a high school situation and its not—this is a transitional
period for these kids from having one teacher to having 5, 6, 7, 8 in a day and
these children are not developmentally, socially, emotionally ready for this
transition, so middle school needs to be an environment where there are

advocates. There are mentors. There is a teaming approach. Where there are two or three teachers that they meet with so relationships can be built ... I see middle schools as taming the beast, and the beast is the middle school child yet their face is still childlike."

In much of her response, Green echoes the rhetoric of the National Middle School Association (NMSA) and other middle school advocates who argue that the middle school model is the "best" way to work with early adolescents. In addition, she shares the perspective that the middle schooler is out of control and must be tamed presumably by a schooling environment designed to do just that. The interesting irony in her description of the middle school student and Denzel's description of Green is that she is the one who acts like a beast who needs someone to tame her, yet she describes the students as beastly.

Similarly, DeGaulle describes the incentive plan she (and Green) used to motivate her students.

DeGaulle (DeG):   ... The kinds of things I need to do with them aren't so much behavioral (inaudible) as they are academic ... Every time they complete a task they get a ticket ...

Interviewer   :   Ok

DeG   :   ...and if they get so many tickets in a week...we have a special reward for them from 2 to 3 on Saturday. Really cool. And if the class does it then it [they] sees it as an achievement [and] then they get this significant reward... and that really modifies what we saw at the beginning as the beginning of the problem... *a lot more primal. A lot more Maslow, a lot more lower on the triangle. Basic survival skills* [emphasis mine] ...

Thus, for DeGaulle, "taming the beast" literally entails training the students using treats and rewards to behave in more acceptable ways. Her explanation for their behaviors is not linked to ontological beliefs about the middle schooler; instead, she locates the "beastly" behaviors with environmental or ecological factors:

Because there are some kids that suffer from malnutrition. There are babies or kids in there that when they were little, their mothers were addicted. They went through it too, and they're still exhibiting some things. And, so, um, the other thing that I think helps ... is *with the population that I teach* [emphasis mine] is changing the activity every 12–15 minutes. Now, I'm not saying it's a perfect world, but the kids who act up, they usually can't do it that day. It's usually something else. That they bring it in their emotional intelligence. Sometimes it's intellect, but usually it's emotional. Sometimes they're overwhelmed emotionally that they can't break it down and tell me what's going on. Or, they can't deal with it appropriately. *And it's not their fault. Nobody showed them* [emphasis mine]. So, with that class I have a bucket of responsibilities that go beyond the academic. So, why we're not responsible for educating the whole child, I don't know. Because nobody's done that. And I only have six hours to do it. Because 16 hours they leave the school and somebody's (inaudible) or not doing anything to reinforce what people are tying to do. It's really hard.

DeGaulle's response is striking. Although she does not adopt the popular construction of the adolescent as being controlled by hormones and therefore unable to control himself or herself (Lesko, 2001), she draws on the cultural deprivation model as an explanation for what she describes as behaviors that are "out of control." Second, she uses the phrase "educating the whole child," a concept generally used to talk about educational experiences that includes not only academics, but also aesthetics and athletics; however, she uses the phrase in reference to addressing malnutrition, drug addiction, and emotional and/or behavior disorders. At no time does DeGaulle refer to a particular child who might be experiencing these issues, but rather casts the net rather widely to include, presumably, all of her students. Just as she applies the books on tape strategy to all of her students, regardless of whether they are able to read independently, she also applies the cultural deprivation theory to explain and perhaps understand her students. As Bonilla-Silva (2003) explains, racist beliefs in this sociohistorical moment do not manifest in explicit epithets, or the "n-word" if you will. Rather, they manifest in beliefs that in many ways place people of color, especially low-income people of color, as deficient, depraved, and lacking. DeGaulle sees herself as her students' savior from the conditions that plague them—poverty, neglectful parenting, poor teaching, and ultimately mental illness.

Because nobody's done that. And I only have [six hours] to do it. Because 16 hours they leave the school and somebody's [doing] or not doing anything to reinforce what people are tying to do. It's really hard ... What the hell their teacher did last year. I don't know, but I think they should be arrested and thrown in jail because now ... it's like cause and effect. Because they were treated in a certain way last year, now they're acting like ... and [I have to] get past that and get to them. Try not to react to their behaviors because that always escalates. *It's kinda like having group therapy every day for these kids* [emphasis mine] ... on any given day they can be perfectly fine, and on another day, they can be screaming out of control. And, I do whatever I can to explain to them why we're doing what we're doing.

In this instance, though DeGaulle does not view the students' misbehaviors as being normative for middle school students, she does view their behaviors as a manifestation of environmental or ecological factors that she must help students overcome through behavior modification and other strategies situated within a behavioral psychology model. DeGaulle sees herself as her students' only option to help them overcome their circumstances. From a CRT perspective, DeGaulle's perspective perpetuates the construction of urban African American students as being victims to a toxic environment. Although her discourse does not explicitly name race, it codes it. Moreover, her remedies do not address the structural inequities that cause malnutrition or poor teaching but rather put the onus on the students to understand what she perceives as bad behavior and "do better."

On the contrary, despite Green's and DeGaulle's description of middle school students, Jamison was Makayla's first choice for middle schools. Despite the school's reputation for violence, Makayla had looked forward to attending Jamison.

AD: So you went to Jamison?

M :   Yes, Ma'am.

AD: And did you want to go to Jamison or did you want to go to another school?

M :   Well, I heard some bad stuff about Jamison and I didn't want to go at first, but I'm used to it. Ain't nothing wrong with Jamison. I mean, shoot, I like the eighth graders.

AD: Now what bad stuff did you hear about Jamison?

M :   That some kids like to jump people ... and people going to the school and shootin'... But I wasn't really worried. I mean, I was worried about it, cause I was scared, but really ... not that bad for me.

AD: So did any of that stuff really happen or...

M :   It did really happen.

AD: Really?

M :   The school got shoot up there.

AD: Really? Last year?

M :   Um hmm.

AD: Um. They had that happen before?

M :   They had that before.

AD: So if you hadn't gone to Jamison, what school would you go to?

M :   Jamison.

AD: You didn't have any other ...

M :   I had no choice.

Although Makayla wanted to go to Jamison, in this exchange, she explains that she had "no choice" but to attend the school. Her mother resisted placing her in the lottery because she wanted Makayla to go to school in her neighborhood and be able to walk to and from school. While Makayla did not live in Peaceful Hamlet, she lived in the surrounding neighborhood. Her walk to and from school took 30 minutes each way. Her mother's insistence on her daughter attending a school in her home neighborhood is an important counter-story that demonstrates the commitments Black parents, especially Black mothers, make to their children's education.

Makayla admitted to initially being scared of Jamison because the students had a reputation of "jumping" or beating up students apparently for no reason. In addition, the school had two incidents of a "lock down"[3] because a student had brought a gun to school. For Makayla, however, Jamison did not fit with its violent reputation. In fact, Makayla would frequently skip class so that she could go to lunch with the eighth graders.

AD: So, so far what do you think about middle school?

M : It's fine.

AD: It's fine.

M : Cause you don't gotta stay in one class. You might have, you might, I mean, even though you might have a class for several blocks, but it's (unintelligible) and then ... boys.

AD: You like the boys?

M : Um hmm. The eighth graders. I don't like the seventh graders...

AD: What don't you like about them?

M : They are like, dead.

AD: What else ... is there anything else you like about middle school? Or, do you like moving around and changing classes? And, you like the other kids? Well, you like the eighth graders. What else do you like?

M : When you get to classes you get to skip.

Thus, for Makayla, the reputation of Jamison as a violent and unfriendly place does not coincide with her experience. Unfortunately, she is not engaged academically and, as a sixth grader, prefers to skip classes than attend them. In some ways, Makayla's preference for skipping class is a commentary on the academic climate of her classes. Although we could dismiss Makayla as being an outlier, she represents the students whom we most need to focus on: the ones who truly find schooling insignificant. Thus, the challenge for urban schools is to find ways to engage the Makaylas who prefer roaming the hallways than sitting in class. In the following exchange, I probe Makayla to explain why she skips class and what her teachers could do to make her stay in class.

> AD: Now, is it that you don't like your classes or you don't like the teachers?
>
> M :   I don't know. It's just that I'll be stretched out and don't be doing, trying to do no work. I just want to play around from being outside cause we don't get enough time or whatever to play around. We'll be in the middle of doing something, messing around with each other and it just annoys me, so I just skip and have just some fun … have another little hour and a half.
>
> AD: So what would make you, what would keep you from skipping class? Is there anything that they could do?
>
> M :   If they make the classes more enjoyable.

Makayla makes a simple request that teachers make learning fun. Her response also provides an important perspective on what students who tune out think about school—that school is an annoyance that lacks the enjoyment that will engage students. Moreover, Makayla's insights provide a necessary counter to the popular construction of African American students and their families as not valuing education. As stated earlier, Makayla's mother was committed to her daughter's education and specifically chose Jamison for Makayla to attend. She wanted her daughter to be able to attend her neighborhood school and not travel out of her neighborhood—a desire of many parents. In this light, Makayla's mother does not fit the stereotype of the unsupportive, disinterested Black parent. In addition, Makayla is not disinterested in school; she is simply bored with what the school is offering her. Unfortunately, teachers and school personnel attributed her chronic skipping to issues with her homelife and what they believed to be a burgeoning and/or misdiagnosed psychological impairment. Rather than examining the classroom practices that contributed to Makayla's dislike for her classes, school personnel sought to locate the issue within Makayla.

What's Race Got to Do With It?

When asked whether she thought that race was an issue in her school in light of the school's demographics—predominantly Black students but predominantly White teachers—Green stated that she was unaware of any issues with race in the larger school setting. Her response is typical of the liberal color-blind discourse in which people claim to not notice racial differences or purposefully address racial differences.

> … I don't know what happens out and about, ok? I only know what happens in my classroom. I don't see racism happening in my classroom. I don't see myself seeing kids any differently and maybe that's a problem that I have, I don't know… but one thing that I do, do is that I find information that or books that will mirror them whether it's a White kid or whatever but I don't purposely hand a book to a child that has a Black person on the front because they're Black, I'm gonna hand that book to anybody.

This particular passage is interesting for two reasons. First, in line with the popular color-blind discourse, Green states that she does not see herself treating her students differently. Like others, Green adheres to a color-blind ideology. Indeed, for many people, making distinctions based on race is taboo. This color-blind discourse exists in a political climate in which the White House and Supreme Court dismiss the impact of race and racism on educational inequality and appropriate the rhetoric of the civil rights movement to further its anti–civil rights agenda.[4] Implicit here is the notion that racism no longer exists. In fact, schools, in many ways, support this idea that the civil rights movement eradicated racism, and it is something that happened in America's past (Bonilla-Silva, 2003). Certainly, for the students in Green's social studies class, racism is always located in historical moments such as the 1960s and the civil rights movement that are in the distant past and have been resolved.

Thus, while Green may not be conscious of her behaviors, her discourse suggests that she does in fact *see* and *treat* them differently. Second, Denzel, Makayla, and other students in the study stated that they explicitly wanted a curriculum that focused on what they described as "Black History." Almost without exception, when asked to describe what more they wanted from their school and what they would have in their own school if they could build one, all of them described a curriculum that included and reflected Black history and culture. Thus, these students would have welcomed explicit overtures by Green to hand them books and materials that focused on Black people. Green's unwillingness to acknowledge and notice race and distribute materials to students that reflected their cultural backgrounds demonstrates the ways in which she is oblivious to her students' desire for a culturally relevant curriculum.

The following response is a more overt example of Green's color-blind discourse:

> Every child needs high expectations and everything else no matter if they are Black, White, Purple, Yellow, or Green. Sometimes we get so hung up on the race issue that we forget that they are students. Now, if we're talking about urban

students vs. suburban vs. rural, you know, I know rural kids that their parents are in jail just like my urban kids are. You look at the individual student and you see what their needs are and you meet their needs. When you start saying, "ok, what do the Black students need?" then you are setting yourself up. You're segregating your own classroom and I'm sorry, that should not be done, nope.

On the surface, Green's response suggests that she is thoughtful about race and racism and is careful not to alienate her students regardless of color. Certainly, her response is in keeping with the color-blind rhetoric; however, the notion that "all" students need the same thing ignores the racialized reality that we all experienced in the United States whereby some are privileged for their race and others are penalized. In addition, given the racialized achievement gap not only in U.S. schools in general but also in Camden in particular, it is unconscionable that Green would not seek to address the specific needs of the students of color in her class. Indeed, it is troubling that Green chose to ignore the importance of cultural congruency in the curriculum, especially for students of color given the abundance of documented research (Gay, 2000; Irvine, 1990; Ladson-Billings, 1994; Lee, 2007).

"You're not a good reader"

Both Green and DeGaulle very narrowly defined literacy as related to print text. When the teachers engaged in writing instruction, it usually consisted of practice on grammar with few opportunities for students to write in different genres. The creative writing activities were generally very limited. A popular assignment was the acrostic poem on a topic selected by the teacher. One of Green's favorite topics was to have students write an acrostic poem about what Africa meant to them.

When asked to discuss her students' preparation for middle school, Green situated her response in terms of students' reading abilities:

… I think academically some of them are [prepared for middle school] academically, [and] some of them aren't only because, uhmm, social promotion. Uhmm, we have students that you know, are learning disabled but they are still reading at a kindergarten level and in sixth grade … Academically, uhh, I would say reading, uhmm, they, uhh, these students know how to decode. They know how to read a word, but they don't understand what they are reading. So much focus in elementary school is that on just how to read the words and not understanding actually, why we're reading this. Also I think, uhm, under that reading category is also nonfiction because in elementary school we focus so much on reading chapter books that we forget how to read a textbook in that nonfiction text form.

Thus, for Green, "reading" is one of the indications of academic readiness and preparation. For Green, reading at the middle school level is no longer for enjoyment, but for information and in her estimation, her students struggle with those skills. Hence, literacy is framed very narrowly and encompasses only reading texts for specific academic purposes.

DeGaulle's perspective on literacy is similar. Where Green makes the distinction between students who are struggling and students who are not struggling, DeGaulle casts all of her students as struggling readers:

> We did a test, you know ... if you look at my diagnostic assessment most of that class ... they're working at the survival level and they're on the *1st or 2nd grade reading level* [emphasis mine]. And these are seventh graders.

Similar to Green, DeGaulle based her perception of her students' "reading ability" on diagnostic tests that measure and norm grade-level reading ability. For DeGaulle, her students are merely trying to "survive" because they cannot read at grade level. This narrow definition of what it means to be literate shapes her perspective on her students in ways that go beyond academics. DeGaulle uses what she believes to be her students' low literacy as an explanation for what she describes as poor behavior.

Both teachers were solely responsible for the literacy materials used in their classrooms. Quite often, the materials were below the students' reading abilities, and generally did not reflect the students' racial identities. Wedded to particular strategies that focused on decoding text or comprehension of superficial details, the teachers did not encourage an interrogation of issues of power, hegemony, and identity in any of the materials they used. Much of the instruction was didactic in the sense that teachers interpreted texts for the students and told them how to process these materials using particular strategies that seemed awkward and forced. For example, Green often asked students to make "text-to-world," "text-to-text," and "text-to-self" connections (using that exact verbiage); however, she often discouraged the students from making authentic connections to texts that would actually reflect their own life experiences. Green often disagreed with the examples students gave and offered what she considered a more "appropriate" response. For example, during one classroom activity on map skills, Green asked the class to describe what they would wear if they were in the desert. Students called out various items with shorts being the most popular. Green's response to each answer was "no." She told the students what she would wear and ended the discussion by telling the students to continue working on their maps. Regardless of what clothing was the appropriate desert attire, the exchange was not instructive. In that instance, Green did not explain directly what clothing was appropriate and why but simply told them what she would wear. Perhaps the students could have deduced from her examples what was appropriate clothing; however, in that instance and given their lack of direct experience in a desert, the students only learned that their opinions and guesses were wrong.

In DeGaulle's classroom, students did not have the occasion to self-select texts because the class read one book in common that was also on cassette tape or compact disc. While she allowed time for a discussion on the text, students did not have the opportunity to "stop the tape" and raise questions or make comments on the reading passage. Generally, worksheets accompanied the books on tape such that the very reading and interpretation of the text was prefabricated. Hence, there were no occasions for organic and authentic reading and literacy experiences in DeGaulle's classroom.

Generally, the teachers expected students to be quiet in class. This insistence on silence contradicts the focus of literacy instruction that presumably is supposed to help students learn how to *communicate*. It was not clear how, when, and with whom the students would communicate when the only opportunities they had to talk in class were when they were called on by the teacher during class discussions. Moreover, when the teachers wanted students to be quiet or reprimanded them for what they saw as inappropriate behavior, they assigned more work. Denzel recognized the relationship between additional assignments and punishment for misbehavior. He described the increase in the work volume as challenging to complete. For Denzel, schoolwork was something one merely completed to satisfy the teacher and not necessarily something that was instructive. Makayla also saw it as busy work and opted out by skipping class or finding ways to leave the classroom. Although the teachers believe that they were "meeting the needs of their students," it is unclear what and whose needs the teachers were in fact meeting.

During one visit in Green's classroom, a young woman shared with one of the graduate students that she hated social studies and language arts intimating that it was because she disliked Green. Green overheard the young woman's statement, unaware that she was being sarcastic and explained to the student that the reason she did not like language arts and social studies was because, "you're not a good reader and this is hard for you, isn't it?" The student rolled her eyes and did not respond to Green's comment. This exchange again exemplifies the negative perceptions that the teachers have of their students.

Setting Agendas in Schools

This chapter addresses following questions: Who gets to set educational agendas? How are they defined? In addition, what alternatives are offered? I argue that while teachers and school districts complain of the restrictive and limiting nature of federal and state educational legislation, at the microlevel of the classroom, it is teachers who set and define the educational agendas for their students. Moreover, this chapter raises the question, how are larger social, economic, and political contexts implicated in different and competing agendas for school reform in the area of literacy instructional practice? I have tried to answer those questions by demonstrating that, within the context of urban schools and specifically within low socioeconomic status communities, the opinions, beliefs, and agendas of those who "know better" overshadow the interests of the students. Given this, I suggest that research within particular communities must examine the ways in which teachers' superficial understanding of "literacy pedagogies" must provide opportunities for students to actively participate in their learning. Moreover, I attribute these practices to the racialized beliefs the teachers have of their students that justify doling out particular kinds of pedagogies that control and limit what students can know and do. In essence, these pedagogies restrict students' access to literacy, thus, illuminating the ways in which literacy as a civil right is a frustrating endeavor for students of color.

Acknowledgments

I would like to thank Kenneth Fasching-Varner, Detra Price-Dennis, Andre J. Patterson, and Sarah Stalter for their help with this project. Special thanks to David E. Kirkland for his insightful comments on an earlier draft of this manuscript.

Notes

1. Based on student enrollment of 54,660 students, Camden Public Schools is the largest school district in its state. In the school year 2006–2007, CPS had 54,660 students (FY2006 Annual Report, Camden Public Schools).
2. In the fall of 2005, Peaceful Hamlet experienced a wave of home invasions. The homeowners were present at the time and the assailant bound them at gunpoint and burglarized the home.

3. During a lock down, police and school administrators literally lock students, faculty, and staff into the school until such time that the local police and school officials determine that it is safe to release everyone.

4. See Chief Justice Roberts' opinion on the *Community Schools v. Seattle School District No.1*, et al. and *Crystal D. Meredith, Custodial Parent and Next Friend of Joshua Ryan McDonald v. Jefferson County Board of Education*, et al.

References

Bonilla-Silva, E. (2003). *Racism without racists: Colorblind racism and the persistence of racial inequality in the United States*. New York: Rowman & Littlefield.

Chapman, T. (2006). Pedaling backward: Reflections of Plessy and Brown in Rockford public schools' de jure sesegregation efforts. In A. Dixson and C. Rousseau (Eds.), *Critical race theory in education: All God's children got a song* (pp. 67–88). New York: RoutledgeFalmer Press.

Crenshaw, K., Gotanda, N., Peller, G., & Thomas, K. (1995). *Critical race theory: The key writings that formed the movement*. New York: The New Press.

DeCuir, J. T., & Dixson, A. D. (June/July 2004). "And nothing of that had ever been mentioned": Using critical race theory as a tool of analysis and desilencing in education. *Educational Researcher, 33*(5), 26–32.

DeCuir, J. & Dixson, A.D. (2004). "So when it comes out,they aren't that surprised that it is there": Using critical race theory as a tool of analysis of race and racism in education. *Educational Researcher, 33*(5), 26–31.

Dixson, A. (2005). Extending the metaphor: Notions of jazz in portraiture. *Qualitative Inquiry, 11*(1), 106–137.

Dixson, A. D., & Rousseau, C. K. (2005). And we are still not saved: Critical race theory in education 10 years later. *Race, Ethnicity and Education, 8*(1), 7–27.

Dixson, A.D. (2006). The fire this time: Jazz, research and critical race theory. In A. D. Dixson and C. K. Rousseau, (Eds.), *Critical race theory in education: All God's children got a song* (pp. 213–232). New York: RoutledgeFalmer Press.

Duncan, G. (2006). Critical race ethnography in education: Narrative, inequality, and the problem of epistemology. Press. In A. D. Dixson & C. K. Rousseau (Eds.), *Critical race theory in education: All God's children got a song* (pp. 191–212). New York, RoutledgeFalmer Press.

Gay, G. (2000). *Culturally responsive teaching: Theory, research, and practice*. New York: Teachers College Press.

Heath, S. B. (1983). *Ways with words: Language, life and work in communities and classrooms*. Cambridge: Cambridge University Press.

Hymes, D. (1964). Toward a theory of ethnography of communication. *American Anthropologist, 66*(6), 1–34.

Irvine, J. J. (1990). *Black students and school failure*. Westport, CT: Greenwood Press.

King, J.E. (1991) Dysconscious racism: Ideology, identity, and the miseducation of teachers, *Journal of Negro Education, 60*(2), 133–146.

Ladson-Billings, G. (1994). *The dreamkeepers: Successful teachers of African American teachers*. San Francisco: Jossey-Bass.

Ladson-Billings, G., & Tate, W. F. (1995). Toward a critical race theory of education. *Teachers College Record, 97*(1), 47–68.

Ladson-Billings, G. (2000). Racialized discourses and ethnic epistemologies. In N. K. Denzin & Y. S. Lincoln (Eds.), *Handbook of qualitative research* (2nd ed., pp. 257–278). Thousand Oaks, CA: Sage.

Lawrence-Lightfoot, S. (1994). *I've known rivers: Lives of loss and liberation.* Reading, MA: Jamison-Wesley.

Lee, C. D. (2003). Why we need to re-think race and ethnicity in educational research. *Educational Researcher, 32*(5), 3–5.

Lee, C. D., Spencer, M. B., & Harpalani, V. (2003). "Every shut eye ain't sleep": Studying how people live culturally. *Educational Researcher, 32*(5), 6–13.

Lee, C. D. (2007). *Culture, literacy and learning: Blooming in the midst of the whirlwind.* New York: Teachers College Press.

Lesko, N. (2001). *Act your Age! A cultural construction of adolescence.* New York: RoutledgeFalmer Press.

Moll, L. (1992). Funds of knowledge for teaching: Using a qualitative approach to connect homes and classrooms. *Theory into Practice, 31*(2), 132–141.

Prendergast, C. (2003). *Literacy and racial justice: The politics of learning after Brown v. Board of Education.* Carbondale: Southern Illinois University Press.

Rousseau, C. K. (2006). Keeping it real: Race and education in Memphis. In A. D. Dixson & C. K. Rousseau (Eds.), *Critical race theory in education: All God's children got a song* (pp. 113–128). New York: RoutledgeFalmer Press.

Tate, W. F. (1997). Critical race theory and education: History, theory and implications. In M. W. Apple (Ed.), *Review of research in education* (Vol. 22, pp. 191–243). Washington, DC: American Educational Research Association.

Yosso, T. (2006). Whose culture has capital?: A critical race theory discussion of community cultural wealth. In A. D. Dixson and C. K. Rousseau (Eds.), *Critical race theory in education: All God's children got a song* (pp. 167–190). New York: RoutledgeFalmer Press.

III

TEACHING FOR SOCIAL JUSTICE

REVISITING PLAYING IN THE DARK:
THE HIDDEN GAMES
OF RACIALIZATION IN LITERACY
STUDIES AND SCHOOL REFORM

CAROL D. LEE

In her chapter "Still_Black @Stanford.edu: A Story of Black Life in the Academy," Gloria Ladson-Billings raises the difficult question of what it means to socialize and apprentice minority students into the culture of educational research. In the field of literacy studies, the Assembly for Research of the National Council of Teachers of English has sought to serve as an intimate and sustaining community for literacy researchers, young and old. In attending Assembly meetings, as a graduate student and later as a new scholar, I had the opportunity to meet senior scholars, to present my evolving research, and to meet peers who were often struggling with issues similar to my own. However, for many of the years since I first began attending in 1989, I was often the only person of color in attendance. I am proud to be a past chair of the Assembly on Research, having cochaired with my friend Peter Smagorinsky. Peter and I organized the 1999 mid-winter conference on Vygotskian Perspectives on Literary Research, which resulted in an edited volume published by Cambridge University Press (Lee & Smagorinsky, 2000).

The topic for the conference on which this book is based was "Literacy as a Civil Right: Reclaiming Social Justice in Literacy Research and Teaching." Our field has much to learn from civil rights activist and mathematician Robert Moses, founder of the Algebra Project (Moses & Cobb, 2001). Moses has argued that mathematical literacy is one of the most important civil rights

of the twenty-first century because it serves as a gatekeeper to fields of sciences and technology. If we look at the fields in which, for example, African
Americans are majoring, it is clear that the numbers in the sciences and engineering are simply unacceptable. These trends hold true for graduate education
as well (see Figure 7.1).

One might ask why numbers in certain major fields of study count. This
looms as a question when the assumption is that the selection of a job or
profession is simply a matter of individual choice. Whether minority status
is based on numbers in relation to a majority or whether it is based on the
structural ability to exert power, minority communities need collective coordination in pivotal areas to strategically navigate their needs as a people. Thus,
I argue that education serves as an opportunity for individual development
that can provide access to capital, particular social networks, knowledge, and
jobs. Equally important, education serves as the engine for the opportunity of
communities to accrue wealth, expand the reach and impact of their social
networks, to deploy knowledge in service of community needs, and to create

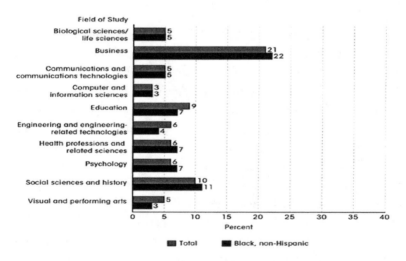

Figure 7.1 Percent of bachelor's degrees conferred in total and to Black, non-Hispanics by
colleges and universities in the top 10 most popular fields of study by field of study:
1999–2000.
Note: Includes 2- and 4-year degree-granting institutions that were participating in Title IV
federal financial aid programs.
Source: U.S. Department of Education, National Center for Education Statistics, Digest of
Education Statistics. 2001, based on Integrated Postsecondary Education Data System (IPEDS).
"Completion" survey 1999–2000.

jobs and businesses as a basis for the accrual of wealth. Because of these possibilities, I believe the strategic concentration in particular professions should be a goal of community development. For people of African descent, this is an international challenge because whether across the diaspora, including the United States, or on the continent itself, we have dire needs that we must become more independent in addressing. Below are those fields of study that I believe are crucial for community development, particularly for communities of African descent.

- Health-related careers
- Engineering
- Urban planning
- Economic development
- Teaching
- Communications
- Law
- History, linguistics, psychology, cognitive science rooted in the African tradition
- Business

You may note here that my line of reasoning about civil rights and social justice may differ somewhat from expectations and the comments in other chapters. I am a bit pessimistic about the idea that communities that struggle for position and power—whether those communities are identified by race and ethnicity, by class, by language, by gender, by sexual orientation, by disability, and so on—can simply depend on the goodwill of others or on the largesse of the government to protect rights and to expand opportunities. I believe that the engine that drives change and responsivity must come from the internal acts of coordination from within the communities in question and from that internal coordination extending to collaborations with other groups on the basis of shared needs and interests. This is my view of the struggle for civil rights in the service of social justice.

The question then emerges about the role of education in terms of this view of civil rights and social justice. I have a three-part answer to that question. The first I have already described; that is, education can serve as the pipeline through which skills in particular domains of knowledge and access to certain jobs and professions are made possible. Second, schools can serve as sites in which young people learn that knowledge serves social functions and in which they can routinely experience the using of knowledge to accomplish social justice ends. This orientation in no way precludes opportunities for knowledge development for individual introspection and personal growth. However, unfortunately, I would argue that in the majority of our schools, and in particular those serving Black and Brown youth and youth from communities of persistent intergenerational poverty, knowledge development rarely takes on either a personal, hermeneutical or a collective social function. This challenge to schooling has important implications for *both* the content of instruction and its organization.

Finally, education, particularly public education, is perhaps the most important site for civic education, for young people to learn how negotiations over power and decision making are possible in a democracy (Gutmann, 1987). Civic education means learning the public narratives about the constitution, the structures of the federal, state, and local governments, how laws are enacted, and about voting and the electoral process. Such information is basic and necessary. At the same time, youth need to learn the underbelly of politics—how special interest groups operate, how media and the strategic deployment of capital exert influence, how organization, persistence, and long-range planning facilitate groups' abilities to stay in the game of jockeying for power and influence.

For each of the functions I have described, critical literacy is one important basis through which people are able to participate in the kinds of activities that such struggles for social justice require. Paulo Freire (1970; Freire & Macedo, 1987) certainly made this argument. Therefore, learning to read and write become resources for civic participation and for collective action. However, the question then arises, reading how and reading what, writing how and writing what. This is the question I want to pursue in this chapter. But I want to first offer a set of warrants for why the particular range of ways of reading and writing are necessary for the social justice ends that I have described, namely ends that facilitate collective growth and development toward meeting the goals articulated within communities. These warrants begin with an analysis of our perennial dance with race.

Analysis of the human genome has revealed that at the level of our gene pools, across so-called racial groups, we are more alike than not (Gould, 1981). We in fact are a common species who have a range of phenotypic markers that capture one very superficial form of our variation. The social significance of these phenotypic markers changes with history and social context. However, for at least the last 500 years, western European countries, which include the United States and Canada, have articulated a philosophy of White supremacy, that is, a presumed supremacy on the basis of skin color (Mills, 1997). Since the 1960s, in response to the impact of the civil rights movement here and the monumental *Brown v. Board of Education* Supreme Court decision, it is not politically correct to discuss or name White supremacy. However, before that, as Gloria Ladson-Billings (2004) so brilliantly noted in her DeWitt Lecture at AERA that was published in *Educational Researcher*, the United States has a longer history of slavery and Jim Crow than of a free state for African Americans and by extension other ethnic minorities; that is, a history of nearly four hundred years of enslavement and nearly hundred years of Jim Crow. During this 500-year history, public and explicit statements regarding White supremacy were evident in public discourse, in the media, in textbooks in schools; and more importantly, in law and in social practice. In graduate school I remember taking the required course in the philosophy of education at the University of Chicago. To be sure, the title of the course was not explicitly an overview of European philosophies of education, but in fact that is exactly what it was. If you didn't know any better, you would assume that the ancient civilizations in China and ancient Kemet (or Egypt), or the indigenous nations of the Americas had no formal conceptions of what it means to be educated or of what functions education should serve. The course also implied that there were no lines of influence from these non-Western civilizations to philosophical thinking about education. We were also required to take a similar course on the history of education, which should also have been simply called a history of European education because that is precisely what we studied. In the history of education course, we read Jack Goody's (1968) account of the civilizations that he claimed had no literacy and therefore no access to the intellective tools for government and economic development. In the philosophy of education course, we read Rousseau (1979) who explicitly said that Negroes had half a brain. I was initially drawn to Rousseau until I encountered the shock of that line. Not only was I the only African American, the only student of color in the class, in my cohort; it never seemed to have even dawned on my professor that this line in Rousseau should even be questioned. I decided that my paper for the class would be to attack Rousseau. As an undergraduate major in English Education at the University of Illinois at Urbana from 1963 to 1966, I was never asked to read even one African American, African, Asian or Asian American, or American Indian text. Not one. Perhaps the saddest testimony was that I never noticed such a glaring omission until some years after I graduated.

I teach two courses on social contexts of learning at Northwestern University. In both courses, I have wonderful students with very interesting life histories.

In 2006, in each class there was one Asian American student. In one class there were two students each of whom has one parent who is Mexican. Beyond that there were no students of color. When I have them read Linda Burton's account of a group of African American adolescents who struggle with the tensions of being parents and assuming adult-like roles at home and being treated more like children when they go to their local high school, I hear great sympathy for these young people; but I also hear comments that indicate a number of students assume that this is a picture of *the* African American community. Their responses are not based on ill will, but on their very limited experiences with people who do not look or live like them. My point with these personal and professional examples is that implicit theories of White supremacy are no less virulent today than they were in the past. Their presence in the world is simply hidden under a polite veneer, under a metalanguage of equality.

This maintenance of implicit assumptions of White supremacy is sustained in part through the very conception of race and its use as a term in our public discourse (Bell, 1992). Any logic that evolves from the construct of race can only lead to a very slippery slope because its very foundation is highly tentative. Race is largely defined on the basis of phenotypic markers. There is no question that there are stark phenotypic differences across human groups. However, these markers exist on a continuum, and there are points along that continuum in which it is difficult to determine on which side one falls in a system of racial classification. What is the precise line of distinction relative to skin color that marks the dark Sicilian as White rather than Black; what are the very dark skinned people of the East Indian subcontinent; how tight must the curl of your hair or the width of your nose or lips be? All of this harkens back to notions of octagoons, that is, classifying people on the basis of what percentage of Black or White blood they had (Haney-Lopez, 1995; Jacobson, 1999; Lee, 2002; Stanton, 1960). The point is if you want to understand human cultures, phenotype is only partially a predictor and a very weak one at that.

A more robust marker of cultural membership is the nature of routine practices, beliefs, and institutional structures, especially the intergenerational character of such practices, beliefs, and institutional structures (Lee, Spencer, & Harpalani, 2003). Such cultural practices are the markers of ethnicity. Regularities in cultural practices, especially those defined by ethnic identification, are powerful (Super & Harness, 1986). This is evident across the world. The ethnic battles after the breakup of the communist block, the tensions between China and Taiwan, the struggles between Igbo and Yoruba in Nigeria are all testimonies to the persistence of ethnic identification across time. This question of ethnic identity within the United States is interesting and a source of our difficulties in understanding and addressing issues of cultural diversity within our country. We have for a long time entertained a grand master narrative of the melting pot, the United States as a place where immigrants elect to come because of unlimited political and economic opportunities; and where when they once come melt into simply being Americans. There is not only some truth to this narrative, but there is also much that it masks. First, every one is not an immigrant, nor a voluntary immigrant. Some of us were already here and were in fact conquered; some of us were forced here in involuntary servitude; some came and still come because the nature of particularly continental politics make economic opportunities within our own borders difficult at best. A great many of us maintain bifurcated identities, maintaining practices, belief systems, institutional structures, and ways of using language that are connected to our countries of origin. This includes involuntary minorities such as people of African descent. It is important to note that the community of people of African descent are quite varied: those who are the descendants of the victims of the African Holocaust of Enslavement; those who are more recent immigrants from the Caribbean, from South and Central America, and from Africa. However, across these communities one can consistently find vestiges of their common African ancestry—in language, in music and dance, in food, in family structures, in beliefs about spirituality, in religious and other rituals, in naming, and so on (K. W. Asante, 1990; M. K. Asante, 1990; Cross, 1991; Hilliard, 1995; King, 1976; Maultsby, 1990; Morgan, 1993; Rickford & Rickford, 1976). At the same time that many of us maintain ethnic identities based on countries of national origin, we also assume identities as Americans. I have found the best way to recognize what we share culturally as Americans is to travel abroad, anywhere.

The points I want to make here are complex, nuanced, and very difficult to wrap our minds around:

- Race is an illogical box that inherently supports implicit theories of White supremacy.
- Ethnicity is a more powerful marker of human cultural communities, one that places people inside history.
- People can and do belong to multiple cultural communities.
- Cultural communities are not static; they have regularities and also undergo change.

So why is all of this important. First, in both the public discourse and in the discourses of our research communities, differences on the basis of assumptions about race are communicated as normative (Graham, 1992; Spencer et al., 2006). We use the terms diverse, multicultural, at-risk, and people of color as ways of capturing particular groups of people. Fundamentally these terms mean "not White." There are the diverse folks, the multicultural folks, the at-risk children, the people of color; and then there are the rest of us, the humans, the normal people. If in fact we did not make these distinctions based on our assumptions about race, then the terms diverse, multicultural, at-risk, and people of color would be used to describe the human condition, to describe all communities. Census data now confirms that our society is more and more diverse. Was it not diverse when even the majority was made up of those from England, Spain, and France; and later from Ireland, Germany, and Italy; and later from Poland and Czechoslovakia? Ironically, the first generation of immigrants felt the country was becoming more "diverse" when their Irish, German, and Italian cousins started arriving in large numbers. In fact, they identified these newcomers as colored (Jacobson, 1999). If the children at Columbine are killing one another, are we not all at risk? With the possible exception of albinos, do we not all have color, have skin tone? However, this is not the broad public understanding of these terms. These terms refer to colored people.

In a similar vein, I sit on many committees reviewing research proposals for funding and studies for publication. I cannot tell you how often the introduction reads something like this: "our society is becoming more diverse; there are all kinds of problems associated with that diversity; we have problems in differences in achievement among the diverse groups; we have the answer to the colored peoples' problems." If you want funding in educational research today, that's your m.o. Focus on diversity. That's why you should get the money or be published. And interestingly, with this ongoing mantra, the percentage of researchers of color getting access to either the funding or the publishing is miniscule. Some have referred to this current state of affairs in educational research as plantation data mining.

So we start from a box with drawers into which we can catalog human communities; we presume these drawers are relatively separate and unidimensional. This classification system assumes a generalized White-people-are-all right and the colored-people-need-help orientation (Gutierrez & Rogoff, 2003; Rogoff, 2003). I often wonder then how we account for the statistic shown in Table 7.1 from National Assessment of Educational Progress (NAEP) data on reading achievement, as one case in point.

Table 7.1 The 1999 NAEP scores for reading achievement 2004 NAEP Performance Levels in Reading for 17-Year-Olds by Race/Ethnicity

Performance Levels	Total	Whites	Blacks	Latino	Other	Black-White Gap
250+	80%	86%	67%	64%	82%	19%
300+	36%	45%	17%	20%	37%	28%
350+	6%	7%	1%	2%	5%	6%

Source: Perle, Moran, Lutkas & Tirre, 2005.

The 1999 NAEP scores for reading achievement have been duplicated in subsequent scores. They suggest that vulnerability in terms of academic achievement in reading, at least, is not limited to minority groups.

So what does all of this have to do with my original propositions? What and how we read as well as what and how we write in school are important elements in our efforts to prepare young people to learn to contribute to the development and empowerment of communities; local organizing is a powerful vehicle for broader issues of social justice and civil rights.

Just as we make inherent value judgments about people and communities informed by our folk beliefs about race, so do we similarly make judgments about knowledge, what is worth knowing, what is worth reading, worth understanding about language that are informed by the same set of beliefs we have about race. That was certainly the case with Rousseau. His views about learning that have been very influential on notions of constructivist learning, learning by doing, were never assumed to be of any value for the Negroes with half a brain and other so-called natives.

In fields of literacy research, we are still very much grounded in hierarchical notions of what narratives count. Classical literature may now include both European, Asian, and African examples (although non-European literature is still on the margins in both the high school and the college-level English course content) (Applebee, 1993); but contemporary rap or classic rap from the past 20 years is not. We continue to use the terms mainstream academic English as the dialect of privilege to which we want to apprentice youth in school (Stotsky, 1999). I don't question its existence or its utilitarian functions. But I also know that there are many circles in which the obtuse "It is I" is not particularly useful and such sites are not simply the street corners in the low-income neighborhoods, but in fact the boardrooms of corporations. So I want to play around with what is often hidden, masked in what we privilege in terms of the literacies that schools teach.

Nobel prize–winning author Toni Morrison (1992) writes a compelling essay called "Playing in the Dark." Here Morrison argues that even though in early American literature one rarely finds characters or plots that involve Blacks, there is a hidden, a masked Black presence in this literature. She argues that it would have been impossible for writers of that era to have had no consciousness about race because these people were living in the midst of slavery; they were living in the midst of the displacement of the indigenous population. She posits that the social norms of the time did not permit them to openly wrestle with their contemporary experiences of race. Therefore, she claims, they instead masked questions of race. Morrison constructs a fascinating interpretation of Melville's White whale in Moby Dick. One of the points here is that in the United States you have to literally bury your head in the sand in order to not face race and all its manifestations. That was the case in Melville's time and it is the case today.

I focus specifically here on response to literature. Literature offers a ripe playing field for interrogating the meanings of race, and by extension of our varying conceptions of what it means to be human, what it means to wrestle with the vagrancies of the human condition. It is this hermeneutic literary portal that provides a point of access for making literature both personal and a vehicle for thinking about questions of social change. There is no question that this is what the great writers do. They use language to create access points for our entry into the subjunctive imaginative worlds they create. In these imaginary worlds, they wrestle with the human condition in all its variation and offer complex possibilities for social change. Although I had read many historical accounts of the African Holocaust of Enslavement, it was not until I read Morrison's (1987) novel Beloved that I had even a glimpse of its human toll. What set of circumstances should lead a mother to see the killing of her baby as a rescue from hell; what set of circumstances could lead a mother to have as her only memory of her many children who had been snatched from her and taken into slavery on other plantations that one of them liked the burnt brown of toast? What was/is the spiritual toll of living with the horrors of what such experiences led you to do, for both the living and the dead, for those who directly experienced the horror and for their children?

Literature, I argue, offers these wonderful opportunities to explore both the uniqueness of human experiences and what we share across cultural communities. I have always been fascinated by the observation of Gabriel Marquez (Bell-Villada, 1990) that he did not know that the stories that his grandmother told him of humans and spirits could be written down until he read the Jewish

German writer Franz Kafka. Magical realism as a genre connects Morrison and Faulkner in the United States, Marquez in South America, and Amos Tutuola in Nigeria. It represents a way of viewing the world, of humans' relationships to the natural world and the world of spirits. It offers explanatory frameworks that can serve important functions for resilience in the face of grave life-course risks. Moreover, interestingly enough, it shares much with the rituals of performance in a storefront Pentacostal church.

In another vein, literature offers wonderful illustrations of how the vernacular languages of everyday experiences, including the code switching across national languages, dialects, and registers, are powerful mediums of communication. Morrison again has written that in the opening of *The Bluest Eye* she was trying to achieve the sense of intimacy that two women, particularly African American women, have in a juicy conversation on the phone. Alice Walker (1983) writes of Celie, the protagonist of *The Color Purple* (Walker, 1982):

> Celie speaks in the voice and uses the language of my step-grandmother, Rachel, an old Black woman I loved. Did she not exist; or in my memories of her, must I give her the proper English of, say, Nancy Reagan?
>
> And I say, yes, she did exist, and I can prove it to you, using the only thing she, a poor woman, left me to remember her by—the sound of her voice. Her unique pattern of speech. Celie is created out of language. In *The Color Purple*, you see Celie because you "see" her voice. To suppress her voice is to complete the murder of her. And this, to my mind, is an attack upon the ancestors, which is, in fact war against ourselves. (Walker, 1983, pp. 63–64)

Literature is a generative ground for the marriage of the everyday and the canonical. Gabriel Marquez has said that his writings in the genre of magical realism reflect the stories he heard from his grandmother, a blend of African and South American influences. He said until he read the Jewish German writer Franz Kafka he did not know that stories like his grandmother's could be written (Bell-Villada, 1990): "When I read that I said to myself, 'Holy shit! Nobody'd ever told me you could do this! That's how my grandma used to tell stories, the wildest things with a completely natural tone" (pp. 72–73). Wayne Booth (1974) notes that irony can be heard in the streets of Bombay as well in the so-called ivory towers. The voices of vernacular languages abound in writers from almost every national tradition: from Zora Neale Hurston and Ralph Ellison in African American literature to Bernard Malamud and Chaim Potok in the Jewish tradition to Federico García Lorca in Spanish national literature. Interestingly Dante Alighieri in the early part of the fourteenth century wrote an essay titled *De Vulgari Eloquentia* arguing for the eloquence

of the vernacular in literature making the case for moving beyond the scholastic tradition of only writing in Latin (Dante, 1996). In African American
literature, the issue of the vernacular in literature is complex, involving not
only uses of dialect by writers such as Paul Laurence Dunbar, Sterling Brown,
Langston Hughes, and Zora Neale Hurston, but also the structural manifestations of jazz and blues motifs in the works of writers such as Jean Toomer,
Ralph Ellison, and Amiri Baraka, to the incorporation of folk motives as
in Toni Morrison's *Song of Solomon* (Jones, 1991). The Black Arts Movement of the 1970s was very much centered on using vernacular language and
African American oral and music traditions in literature (Gabbin, 2004;
Neal, 1989).

So we have seen in my brief examples how and *what* we read can matter
for what kinds of opportunities we and our students have for, as Mica Pollock
(2005) puts it, wrestling with race, for confronting our limited assumptions
and stereotypes about what it means to be human, for guideposts in navigating
the incessant sources of risk that all human life presents to us, for insights into
the tolls of struggles for justice and empowerment. Still, even these examples implicitly suggest that the literature through which we can accomplish
such ends is the classical literature, even when we extend its national borders
beyond Europe. That too represents a certain elitism. I want to put on the table
that there are other medium of narratives that also offer similar hermeneutic
opportunities. Current and classic rap, video, and films also offer opportunities to explore how language is used as a tool, social commentaries on current
conditions, and insights into the human condition. My friends Ernest Morrell
(2002), Maisha Fisher (2003), Jabari Mahiri (2000/2001), Jeff D'Andrade
(Morrell & D'Andrade, 2002), and Shuaib Meacham (1998) are doing excellent research on the aesthetics of contemporary rap as vehicles for literacy
instruction.

In our work in Cultural Modeling, my colleagues and I have begun to
examine what is entailed in comprehending rap as texts (Lee, 1993, 1995,
2000, 2001, 2007). I want to very briefly share some of that work with you
to buttress my overarching argument for literacy teaching in schools as an
instrument for expanding opportunities for youth to learn to contribute to the
development of communities. From a most basic level, learning to read well
in any discipline or genre is useful for general reading abilities, and general
reading abilities are highly predictive of academic success broadly speaking.
In a related vein, the kind of reflection on life, on what it means to be adap-
tive to life's circumstances, I would argue has value in long-term goal setting

and the coordination of efforts to persist in pursuit of those goals; and that routine experiences with worlds (imaginary and real) in which people are connected to communities and see their life efforts as contributing to those communities—together increase the likelihood that a young person would envision a future in which he or she did more than dream of accruing personal wealth. Please understand that I am not advocating a Pollyanna version of reading biographies of successful people or stories of uncomplicated lives.

I want here to illustrate how the skills entailed in understanding the symbolism in Morrison's *Beloved* are similar to those entailed in understanding "The Mask" by the Fugees as an example. (see Table 7.2)

Table 7.2 illustrates how a common set of strategies and heuristics can be deployed to deconstruct a canonical and a popular text. For me, there is a great irony that there are so many points of convergence between what we as a field identify as the mainstream, the classic, the literary, and what we by default identify as nonmainstream, popular, and in fact ghetto. These unmarked lines of divergence that we create through our practices—textbooks, curriculum, assessments, pedagogical strategies—have at their roots the same assumptions about race, about an implied sense of White supremacy

Table 7.2 Strategies for Interpreting Symbolism in Literature and Everyday Practice

	Everyday Practice	Subject Matter
Task	Interpreting rap lyrics with symbolism	Interpreting symbols in Toni Morrison's Beloved
	Reasoning	
Strategies	• Notice where the author gives attention • Reject a literal interpretation • Identify passages within and across sections where there is textual detail about what you have noticed • Infer similarities across those details • Brainstorm about real world connections to those details and similarities you have drawn across details • Construct an explanation that links your real world associations and the patterns you have inferred abut the textual details you noticed	
Heuristics	• Assume examples are related	
Habits of Mind and Dispositions	• Attend to language play as an aesthetically pleasing end in itself • Be playful in one's reasoning	

Source: Lee, 2007.

that inform our labels for diversity and our constant dance with difference. If we are to ward against our calls for social justice as a masked march for all to join the ranks where White is right, where mainstream is sameness, where even Whiteness is undifferentiated, where power remains in the hands of an elite, and where life-course outcomes remain predictable by race and class, and by gender within race and class, then as a community of literacy scholars, we must advocate new practices; we must wrestle with our own internal assumptions. I am a past president of NCRLL, the National Conference of Research on Language and Literacy. I recently looked at one of the books in the NCRLL series on research methods: *On Qualitative Inquiry: Approaches to Language and Literacy Research* (Kamberelis & Dimitriadis, 2005). I have great respect for the authors and am highly appreciative of the series. However, as I began to read through the volume and examine the index, it occurred to me—there are virtually no African American, Latino, Asian American, or American Indian scholars referenced in this volume. The analysis, although quite thorough, is another grand master narrative of European intellectual history. NCRLL is going to publish a volume by Arlette Willis (in press) of the University of Illinois at Urbana who documents a history of critical theoretical approaches that captures the rich contributions from across communities to questions of critical theory. My point here is that the implied master narrative of White supremacy is not simply a far off litany among those we consider the political conservatives. It is alive and well in our midst. As Toni Morrison would say, we too are playing in the dark and often not acknowledging the web of assumptions that mask us.

Conclusions

Assumptions of privilege pervade the social and intellectual organization of our school curricula. This is equally prevalent in the field of literacy studies as in other areas of study. If we are to integrate social justice ends into the literacy curricula including socialization into the discipline from k-12 through graduate education, we need nuanced views of what constitutes disciplined ways of reading and writing, in part, so that our efforts to reformulate the curriculum are not rooted in simplistic idealistic notions of cultural relevance and multiculturalism. Such reformulations must be rooted in deep disciplinary connections if literacy education is to provide potential access to knowledge and social networks that can support community empowerment.

References

Applebee, A. (1993). *Literature in the secondary school: Studies of curriculum and instruction in the United States (NCTE Research Report No. 25)*. Urbana, IL: National Council of Teachers of English.

Asante, K. W. (1990). Commonalities in African dance: An aesthetic foundation. In M. K. Asante & K. W. Asante (Eds.), *African culture: The rhythms of unity* (pp. 71–82). Trenton, NJ: Africa World Press.

Asante, M. K. (1990). The African essence in African-American language. In M. K. Asante & K. W. Asante (Eds.), *African culture: The rhythms of unity* (pp. 233–252). Trenton, NJ: Africa World Press.

Bell, D. (1992). *Faces at the bottom of the well: The permanence of racism*. New York: Basic Books.

Bell-Villada, G. (1990). *Garcia Marquez: The man and his work*. Chapel Hill: University of North Carolina Press.

Booth, W. (1974). *A rhetoric of irony*. Chicago: University of Chicago Press.

Burton, L., Allison, K., & Obeidallah, D. (1995). Social context and adolescents: Perspectives on development among inner-city African-American teens. In L. Crockett & A. Crouter (Eds.), *Pathways through adolescence: Individual development in social contexts*. Mahway, NJ: Lawrence Erlbaum.

Campbell, J. R., Hombo, C. M., & Mazzeo, J. (2000). *NAEP 1999 trends in academic progress: Three decades of student performance*. Washington, DC: National Center for Educational Statistics.

Cross, W. (1991). *Shades of black: Diversity in African American identity*. Philadelphia: Temple University Press.

Dante, A. (1996). *Dante: De vulgari eloquentia* (S. Botterill, Trans.). New York: Cambridge University Press.

Fisher, M. T. (2003). Open mics and open minds: Spoken word poetry in African diaspora participatory literacy communities. *Harvard Education Review, 73*(3), 362–389.

Freire, P. (1970). *Pedagogy of the oppressed*. New York: Herder & Herder.

Freire, P., & Macedo, D. (1987). The illiteracy of literacy in the United States. In P. Freire & D. Macedo (Eds.), *Literacy: Reading the world and the world* (pp. 120–140). South Hadley, MA: Bergom & Garvey Publishers.

Gabbin, J. (Ed.). (2004). *Furious flower: African American poetry from the black arts movement to the present*. Charlottesville: University of Virginia Press.

Goody, J. (1968). *Literacy in traditional societies*. New York: Cambridge University Press.

Gould, S. J. (1981). *The mismeasure of man*. New York: Norton.

Graham, S. (1992). Most of the subjects were white and middle class: Trends in published research on African Americans in selected APA journals, 1970–1989. *American Psychologist, 47*(5), 629–639.

Gutierrez, K., & Rogoff, B. (2003). Cultural ways of learning: Individual traits or repertoires of practice. *Educational Researcher, 32*(5), 19–25.

Gutmann, A. (1987). *Democratic education*. Princeton, NJ: Princeton University Press.

Haney-Lopez, J. (1995). The social construction of race. In R. Delgado (Ed.), *Critical race theory: The cutting edge*. Philadelphia: Temple University Press.

Hilliard, A. G. (1995). *The maroon within us: Selected essays on African American community socialization*. Baltimore, MD: Black Classic Press.

Jacobson, M. (1999). *Whiteness of a different color: European immigrants and the alchemy of race.* Cambridge: Harvard University Press.

Jones, G. (1991). *Liberating voices: Oral tradition in African American literature.* New York: Penguin Books.

Kamberelis, G., & Dimitriadis, G. (2005). *Qualitative inquiry: Approaches to language and literacy research.* New York: Teachers College Press & National Conference on Language and Literacy.

King, J. R. (1976). African survivals in the black community: Key factors in stability. *Journal of Afro-American Issues, 4*(2), 153–167.

Ladson-Billings, G. (2004). Landing on the wrong note: The price we paid for Brown. *Educational Researcher, 33*(7), 3–13.

Lee, C. D. (1993). *Signifying as a scaffold for literary interpretation: The pedagogical implications of an African American discourse genre.* Urbana, IL: National Council of Teachers of English.

Lee, C. D. (1995). A culturally based cognitive apprenticeship: Teaching African American high school students' skills in literary interpretation. *Reading Research Quarterly, 30*(4), 608–631.

Lee, C. D. (2000). Signifying in the zone of proximal development. In C. D. Lee & P. Smagorinsky (Eds.), *Vygotskian perspectives on literacy research: Constructing meaning through collaborative inquiry* (pp. 191–225). New York: Cambridge University Press.

Lee, C. D. (2001). Is October Brown Chinese: A cultural modeling activity system for underachieving students. *American Educational Research Journal, 38*(1), 97–142.

Lee, C. D. (2002). Interrogating race and ethnicity as constructs in the examination of cultural processes in developmental research. *Human Development, 45*(4), 282–290.

Lee, C. D. (2007). *Culture, literacy and learning: Blooming in the midst of the whirlwind.* New York: Teachers College Press.

Lee, C. D., & Smagorinsky, P. (Eds.) (2000). *Vygotskian perspectives on literacy research: Constructing meaning through collaborative inquiry.* New York: Cambridge University Press.

Lee, C. D., Spencer, M. B., & Harpalani, V. (2003). Every shut eye ain't sleep: Studying how people live culturally. *Educational Researcher, 32*(5), 6–13.

Mahiri, J. (2000/2001). Pop culture pedagogy and the end(s) of school. *Journal of Adolescent & Adult Literacy, 44*(4), 382–386.

Maultsby, P. K. (1990). Africanisms in African-American music. In J. E. Holloway (Ed.), *Africanisms in American Culture* (pp. 185–210). Bloomingdale: Indiana University Press.

Meacham, S. (1998). Threads of a new language: A response to Eisenhart's "On the subject of interpretive review." *Review of Educational Review, 68*(4), 401–407.

Mills, C. (1997). *The racial contract.* Ithaca, NY: Cornell University Press.

Morgan, M. (1993). The Africaness of counterlanguage among Afro-Americans. In S. Mufwene (Ed.), *Africanismsm in Afro-American Language Varieties.* Athens: University of Georgia Press.

Morrell, E. (2002). Toward a critical pedagogy of popular culture: Literacy development among urban youth. *Journal of Adolescent & Adult Literacy, 46*(1), 72–78.

Morrell, E., & D'Andrade, J. (2002). Promoting academic literacy with urban youth through engaging hip-hop culture. *English Journal, 91*(6), 88–93.

Morrison, T. (1987). *Beloved.* New York: Alfred A. Knopf.

Morrison, T. (1992). *Playing in the dark: Whiteness and the literary imagination.* Cambridge, MA: Harvard University Press.

Moses, R. P., & Cobb, C. E. (2001). *Radical equations: Math literacy and civil rights.* Boston: Beacon Press.

Neal, L. (1989). *Visions of a liberated future: Black arts movement writings.* New York: Thunder's Mouth Press.

Perle, M., Moran, R., Lutkas, A., & Tirre, W. (2005). *NAEP 2004 trends in academic progress: Three decades of student performance in reading and mathematics.* Washington, DC: National Center for Education Statistics, U.S. Department of Education, Institute of Education Sciences.

Pollock, M. (2005). *Colormute: Race talk dilemmas in an American school.* Princeton, NJ: Princeton University Press.

Rickford, J., & Rickford, A. (1976). Cut-eye and suck teeth: African words and gestures in new world guise. *Journal of American Folklore, 89*(353), 194–309.

Rogoff, B. (2003). *The cultural nature of human development.* New York: Oxford University Press.

Rousseau, J. J. (1979). *Emile, or on education.* New York: Basic Books.

Spencer, M. B., Harpalani, V., Cassidy, E., Jacobs, C., Donde, S., Goss, T., et al. (2006). Understanding vulnerability and resilience from a normative development perspective: Implications for racially and ethnically diverse youth. In D. Chicchetti & E. Cohen (Eds.), *Developmental Psychopathology* (pp. 627–672). Hoboken, NJ: Wiley Publishers.

Stanton, W. (1960). *The leopard's spots: Scientific attitudes toward race in America, 1815–59.* Chicago: University of Chicago Press.

Stotsky, S. (1999). *Losing our language: How multicultural classroom instruction is undermining our children's ability to read, write, and reason.* New York: Free Press.

Super, C. M., & Harness, S. (1986). The developmental niche: A conceptualization at the interface of child and culture. *International Journal of Behavioral Development, 5,* 545–569.

Walker, A. (1982). *The color purple.* New York: Simon & Schuster.

Walker, A. (1983). *In search of our mother's gardens: Womanist prose by Alice Waker.* New York: Harcourt Brace Jovanovich.

Willis, A. (in press). *On critically conscious research—Arlette Willis.* New York: National Conference of Research on Language and Literacy. Teachers College Press.

· 8 ·

LANGUAGE AND LITERACIES
AS CIVIL RIGHTS

KRIS GUTIERREZ

Colonialism is not satisfied merely with holding a people in its grip and emptying the Native's brain of all form and content; by a kind of perverted logic, it turns to the past of the oppressed people and distorts, disfigures, and destroys it.

—(Biko, 1978, p. 29).

Nondominant people in the United States currently live in a neocolonial condition in which they experience socioeconomic, educational, linguistic, and cultural repression. Historically, restricting and regulating a community's language practices has served as a means for dismembering people from their history, as well as a history of their practice. Recognizing the important role language plays in helping communities sustain their link to the past, to valued practices and identities, helps us understand why language and literacy must be conceived of as civil rights.

In this chapter, I examine the politics of race and class in the schooling of students from poor, nondominant communities in the United States, the ideologies at work in educational policies and practices, including the ways language and literacy, and ability function as educational proxies that sustain privilege for students from dominant groups through color-blind, merit-based interventions. For example, consider that students who experience schooling in increasing deplorable and inequitable learning environments are held to the same measures of accountability as their more privileged counterparts.

Undergirded by a fictitious meritocracy in which significant inequality across institutions and their practices is accepted as a function of hard work, ability, competence, and motivation, the discourse around school reform increasingly essentializes what counts as education and learning, as well as the learner and his or her community's practices.

As I have written elsewhere, contemporary theorizations of nondominant communities often work hand and glove with reductive and static notions of culture and poverty to construct and employ deficit, classist, and racist explanations of the "underachievement" of nondominant students, especially in core subject areas such as literacy (Gutiérrez & Arzubiaga, under review); Gutiérrez & Rogoff, 2003). Such explanations link the "failure" of nondominant students with the "failure" of their schools and communities, without accounting for the history of pervasive social and educational inequities experienced by nondominant communities. Moreover, the ideologies at work in the constructs of success and achievement also help create the very inequalities that result in low-performing schools and the "underachievement" of students from nondominant communities who populate these schools. This enduring inequity is not solely an educational problem; it is at its core a moral question.

This immorality of inequality in American schooling—with its arrogant and blatant disregard for the "other"—has been obscured by a history of *White innocence* instantiated in a "sameness as fairness" ideology informing past and current educational reform and the public discourses (Crosland, 2004; Gutiérrez & Jaramillo, 2006). By proposing new forms of equal educational opportunity through a color-blind meritocracy, the link between economic and educational disparities, power relations, and historically racialized practices is obfuscated. I draw on Gotanda's (2004) theorization of White innocence[1]—a racialized analytic concept that served as the standpoint from which Gotanda examined racial ideology in the *Brown v. Board of Education* decision. In his analysis, Gotanda argues that the U.S. Court was engaged in defending and, thus, maintaining White innocence by explaining the decision to overturn segregation as the result of new scientific evidence of the detrimental psychological effects of segregation on Blacks. Specifically, by claiming that the "new" empirical findings regarding psychological damage to Blacks constituted previously unavailable scientific information about the effects of segregation, the Court was able to claim "Who knew that segregation was harmful to Blacks!" (Thank goodness for science!) and absolve itself of any complicity with the legacy of racist practices and, ultimately, remain "innocent" (Gutiérrez, 2006; Gutiérrez & Jaramillo, 2006).

I have elaborated this concept in my own work (in collaboration with Gotanda) to illustrate how neoliberal and neoconservative policies work with impunity to preserve a meritocracy that limits the possibility of ever-achieving equity in our educational system.[2] Absent any analysis of the role inequities play in schooling and academic performance, policy makers, educational scientists, and publishers, for example, easily advance notions of achievement as unproblematic, where achievement is a function of individual effort, intelligence, and performance on normed, standardized tests, and the like. Within this perspective, the practices of middle-class families serve as the normative backdrop for school achievement.

Consistent with these views, deficit ideologies and reductive notions of culture and cultural communities are pervasive in this country's discourse and are deeply embedded in notions of success, excellence, and merit. At the same time, devaluing the cultural, social, symbolic, and intellectual capital of nondominant communities minimizes any threat to dominant communities and institutions and the meritocracy, and marginalizes and problematizes the difference.

As the face of the United States changes, the cultural warriors are increasingly vocal about the threat that the "difference" poses to the American culture. The cultural war, according to Bill O'Reilly's (the self-proclaimed cultural warrior) Web site (http://www.billoreilly.com/culturewarrior), "[is defined as a war] between those who embrace traditional values and those who want to change America into a 'secular-progressive' country. In [his] book he clearly fights the good fight for the soul of America." This soul of America is a monolithic, monolingual soul that is intolerant to diversity and difference of any kind.

Lamenting a fictionalized past and reifying a monolithic culture are hallmark strategies of the cultural warrior. In a recent book, *One Nation, One Standard: An Ex-Liberal on How Hispanics Can Succeed Just Like Other Immigrant Groups*, Herman Badillo (2006), a once prominent Latino politician, illustrates how deficit-oriented ideologies are at work across communities, even in nondominant communities themselves. In his book, Badillo provides an elaborated, bootstraps argument about the root cause of the underachievement of the Latino community in the United States. According to Badillo,

> Hispanics have no one to blame but themselves for the disastrous high-school dropout rates of the younger members of their community ... Whenever a child is left behind, it is not the fault of the teachers, or the principals, of the school chancellor, or the mayor, or the president. It is their fault. (p. 51)

Sustaining pathological narratives of nondominant communities helps preserve the idea that an equitable system built on true merit, ability, and hard work rather than power and wealth exists in this country. Such ideologies are grounded in ahistorical, incomplete, racialized, and classed understandings of underachievement of nondominant communities.

Preserving the myth of a meritocratic educational system as a neutral and color-blind institution also allows policy makers, both neoliberal and neoconservative, to promote a "common culture" and "common curriculum" under the "sameness as fairness" banner. By utilizing a pseudo-equity framework, those in power detach themselves from current and historical discriminatory practices in the schooling of nondominant students. Their "innocence" intact, no fundamental structural change in the legacy of cultural, social, and institutional racism in the United States is required or occurs. Moreover, once again, a generation of students from nondominant communities becomes the collateral damage of policies in which equity is trumped by marketplace principles of efficiency, accountability, quality, and choice.

Normalizing Inequity: Regulating Language

In many regions of the country marked by new demographic shifts, anti-immigrant sentiments and educational reform policies work together to normalize the underachievement of nondominant students, especially immigrant students, and their dramatically inequitable learning conditions. Guided by the "sameness as fairness" principle and its color-blind policies, the new federalized literacy program promotes a normative view of children living in poverty, their learning needs, and their communities' language practices. Under these initiatives, children from nondominant communities, including English Learners, are still most likely to receive a one-size-fits-all approach to language and literacy learning, even though they have a range of learning strengths and needs. Here language becomes a proxy for race and ethnicity and serves as the tool for organizing schooling around a "sameness as fairness" principle that helps ensure new forms of segregation and inequity. Further, these English-only and one-size-fits-all programs not only expose students to the most restrictive literacy diet and limit the use of students' full linguistic toolkit in the service of learning, they also attempt to erase differences that matter.

As I argued earlier in this chapter, language and literacy practices are key sites for regulating the difference, as an individual's and communities' identities are indexed in their valued language and literacy practices. As Ochs and Schieffelin (1989) wrote some time ago, language has a heart and, I would argue, a soul that is imbued with the repertoire of experience appropriated in the cultural practices with valued others in one's communities. Language and other communicative practices, thus, are permeated with the beliefs, values, orientations, and ideologies. Theories of language ideology (Gal, 1992; Kroscrity, 2004) are particularly instructive in helping us understand that ideologies[3] (language and otherwise) are indexed in the individual and group's language practices. Moreover, ideologies cannot be disentangled from the social, political, and economic interests of the nation-state (Razfar, 2005, p. 405). From this perspective we can begin to understand how English-only ideologies, xenophobic discourses, and anti-immigrant sentiments combine national and local immigration debates and ideologies with color-blind and meritocratic educational policies to normalize the way we conceive of poor children, immigrant children, their linguistic practices, and the education and everyday life they deserve.

Language Ideologies and Immigrant Rights

Normalizing language has served as an object of the cultural wars, especially around issues of immigration. This link between language policies and immigration has had a long history in the United States. For example, in the latter half of the twentieth century, Senator S. I. Hayakawa and Dr. John Tanton founded the U.S. English Foundation—an organization designed to promote English as the official language. Tanton had been the head of the Zero Population Growth and the founder of the Federation for American Immigration Reform (FAIR), an anti-immigration group (http://www.us-english.org/foundation/). Crawford (1996) has also examined this link and argued the following:

> Consider the close, but frequently denied, connections between language restrictionists and immigration restrictionists. At one time or another, US English and the Federation for American Immigration Reform (FAIR) have shared a suite of offices, a general counsel, a direct-mail wizard, a political-action-committee director, a writer-publicist, several rich contributors, and Dr. Tanton himself as founder and chairman. Yet each group has repeatedly disclaimed any association with the other. (p. 15)

Standardizing a community's language is a key strategy in the cultural wars today and has been so historically as well. Consider Theodore Roosevelt's's infamous remarks about the role of English in cultural maintenance:

> We have room for but one language in this country, and that is the English language, for we intend to see that the crucible turns our people out as Americans, of American nationality, and not as dwellers in a polyglot boarding-house. ([1919] 1926: XXIV, 554, as cited in Crawford, 1996)

More recently, the link between language ideologies and new or expanding language communities that differ from our own has become more transparent, as anti-immigrant hysteria and the xenophobia resulting from the "rising brown wave" of immigrants have heightened attempts to normalize a community by regulating its language practices.

In addition, nowhere is the cultural war around language being played out more fiercely than on the educational terrain. In schooling contexts with large numbers of students from nondominant communities, the struggle has everything to do with what students read, write, in what language, with which literacies, as well as whose stories can be told. On a larger scale, anti-immigrant ideologies are institutionalized in the current federalized literacy program that, in its discourse and instantiation, becomes the means for socializing large numbers of people toward a new language ideology, as well as for promoting deficit ideologies about immigrant communities. Moreover, students' home language practices serve as the rationale for sorting children into categories and curricular programs that de-emphasize meaning making and critical thought in any language.

Sounding American: Developing Sameness as Fairness

Our language practices serve as a marker of our identity and the status afforded our language by dominant communities. One strategy for leveling the community toward a "common culture" is to try to eradicate any vestiges of nondominant communities' cultural past and the cultural artifacts that mediate everyday life. For example, if you travel across many neighborhoods in Los Angeles, you are likely to see flyers posted on billboards and light posts advertising courses that will help nonnative speakers of English lose their accents. The signs read, "Speak English Like an American," or they advertise courses in "Foreign accent reduction," or "accent modification"; or one can buy a book that promises to help eliminate or reduce "other-than-English" accents in a month. Of course, some accents are more readily accepted than others.[4] The idealized language of the United States has neither accent nor nonstandard forms of language use. Indeed, as Wolfenstein (1993) has argued:

> Languages have skin colors. There are white nouns and verbs, white grammar and white syntax. In the absence of challenges to linguistic hegemony, indeed language is white. If you don't speak white you will not be heard, just as when you don't look white you will not be seen. (p. 331)

Sounding American is one means toward erasing difference, whether it comes from accent reduction programs or drilling children to learn English phonics in isolation of rich literacy practices and texts in either English or the home language. Language-planning scholar Richard Ruiz (qtd. in Gutierrez, et al., 2002) has argued that phonics-based reading programs in which children who are English Learners are drilled in isolated word sounds is a language-planning issue, not solely a curricular issue:

> In programmatic terms, if you can make ELLs sound more like normative English speakers with the short-term gains that you get from phonics programs, you can exit them of primary-language programs more quickly. (2002, p. 336)

Standardized, one-size-fits-all language programs, organized around the acquisition of phonemic awareness in English and normative views of language help ensure that nonnative speakers of English "sound American." In this way, the erasure of practices and identities that matter begins, in part, in literacy programs that attempt to normalize students through language practices that are not oriented toward powerful literacies (Crowther, Hamilton, & Tett, 2001; Street, 1995). I return to the notion of powerful literacies shortly.

Moreover, attention to how the language ideologies at work in such narrowly conceived English-only literacy practices promote the loss of the home language is largely absent in discussions of the consequences of socially engineered literacy programs. And while Lou Dobbs and others signal the alarm of "broken borders" and the demise of "civilization as we know it," the demographic data regarding home language maintenance are clear. By the third generation, as Rumbaut (2006) has documented, English has replaced the home language in use. However, if the trend in providing English Learners an impoverished literacy diet persists, we may well have generations of students who not only have learned to decode nonsense syllables but also have lost the opportunity to extend their literacy practices and the social, economic, and cultural benefits of bilingualism and biliteracies.

Students' Right to Their Own Language: Students' Right to Learn

The ever-increasing divide between rich and poor, between dominant and nondominant communities, is exacerbated in educational contexts with significant numbers of immigrant children. In these settings, the pressure on educators to increase standardized test scores creates a context in which English becomes the default language across all instructional activities (Gutiérrez, et al., 2002). The challenge for literacy educators is daunting; at the same time, there is an extraordinary opportunity for progressive educators to take a stand against repressive language and literacy practices and policies and support students' right to the use of their full linguistic toolkit as learners and valued meaning makers in school and elsewhere.

We should take a lesson from the Conference on College Composition and the bold, instructive, and ethical stance their Board took in 1975 when they passed a resolution on "Students' Right to Their Own Language":

> We affirm the students' right to their own patterns and varieties of language—the dialects of their nurture or whatever dialects in which they find their own identity and style. Language scholars long ago denied that the myth of a standard American dialect has any validity. The claim that any one dialect is unacceptable amounts to an attempt of one social group to exert its dominance over another. Such a claim leads to false advice for speakers and writers, an immoral advice for humans. A nation proud of its diverse heritage and its cultural and racial variety will preserve its heritage of dialects. We affirm strongly that teachers must have the experiences and training that will enable them to respect diversity and uphold the right of students to their own language. (Committee on CCC Language Statement, 1975, pp. 710–711)

We need to revive and expand this resolution to address students' right to learn in their own language, their right to show their competence in the language that best demonstrates what they know, and to use their language in sense-making activity. Ensuring this right is also a responsibility of educators and researchers. Freire's (1998) words are instructive here,

> I cannot be a teacher if I do not perceive with even greater clarity that my practice demands of me a definition of where I stand. A break with what is not right ethically.

I must choose between one thing and another thing. I cannot be a teacher and be in favor of everyone and everything. I cannot be in favor merely of people, humanity, vague phrases far from the concrete nature of educative practice. Mass hunger and unemployment, side by side with opulence, are not the result of destiny. (Freire 1998, p. 93)

The shift toward transformative teaching requires literacy educators and researchers, and policy makers to reframe the way English Learners and students from nondominant communities and their language practices are conceptualized. Similarly, literacy education must be redefined as part of a transformative educational agenda. Within this agenda, "powerful literacies" become the object of literacy activities in schools and supportive learning environments.

Here I use the notion of "powerful literacies" to refer to several kinds of literacy. First, there are the hegemonic literacies practices of institutions; these powerful literacies are both dominant and dominating, bolstered by marketplace reforms that define the federalized education, particularly literacy, agenda. As Hamilton (1997) has noted, such literacy practices are steeped in histories of practices of domination; these are authoritarian literacies imbued with relations of power. In addition, therefore, such literacies have been used both to maintain privilege and marginalize the *other*. The conceptualization of powerful literacies advanced here ruptures the hegemony of monolithic institutionalized literacies.

Like Crowther and colleagues (2001), I also use "powerful literacies" to describe the "alternative" literacies that are excluded from institutionalized literacies. These vernacular literacies found in everyday practices are not only robust in their own right, but they also serve as generative tools for meaning making and critical social thought. From a cultural historical perspective, everyday literacies illuminate the forms of horizontal learning that occur as people travel across settings, tasks, and boundaries; that is, what gets learned in this movement across practices (Engeström, 2003; Gutierrez, 2005).

The related concept of "repertoires of practice" (Gutiérrez & Rogoff, 2003) may be a useful way to think about the toolkit that people develop over time, space, and history. Specifically, the notion of "repertoires of practice" helps us rethink learning beyond the binaries of home/school or formal/informal, as dichotomizing students' experience makes it more difficult to capture the "horizontal" expertise that people develop across everyday practices. For example, consider what children learn as they translate for their parents across business and social institutions and practices, traverse national borders, provide sibling care, and negotiate new cultural practices. Traditional notions of development usually refer to change along a vertical dimension such as the development from immaturity and incompetence to maturity and competency (Engeström, 1996, p. 6); vertical notions of development do not account for the complexity of students' everyday life and the learning therein.

Schools necessarily have been about the accumulation of subject matter knowledge over time—what might be called "vertical" expertise (Engeström, 1996). Institutional forms of literacy learning are conceptualized as vertical expertise. I believe the notion of repertoires of practice helps us attend both to vertical and horizontal forms of expertise; this includes not only what students learn in formal learning environments such as schools but also what they learn participating in a range of practices outside of school. In my work, I conceptualize a sociocritical literacy as a powerful hybrid literacy, as it is constitutive of both vertical and horizontal forms of learning. As I elaborate shortly, a sociocritical literacy is also a historicizing literacy, as it privileges and is contingent upon the students' sociohistorical lives, both proximally and distally. Thus, in our work with youth from nondominant communities, we emphasize the development of sociocritical literacies in which everyday and institutional literacies are reframed to encompass a broader notion of what counts as literacy and academic literacy—one that is oriented toward critical social thought. In contrast, current forms of academic and school literacies to which students have access are ahistorical, emphasize vertical learning, and are oriented toward weak literacies.

Toward a Sociocritical Literacy

Teaching for transformation is especially difficult in hard times in which creating robust learning communities goes against the grain established by the "sameness as fairness" framework. I take this opportunity to share some principles that disrupt this paradigm—principles that both grow out of and guide my work with English Learners, students from migrant farmworker backgrounds, and students from nondominant communities in general. First, the object of a rigorous, equity-oriented pedagogical ecology is learning, not teaching, and in this way, this context has the potential to be transformative for all its participants. Realizing this potential requires understanding that the participants of learning communities have a range of cultural practices, viewpoints, and subjectivities. However, instead of focusing on the differences between students' home and schooling practices (a move that often leads to deficit and delimiting conceptualizations), a more productive approach focuses on and extends the repertoires of practice that students develop as they participate in the valued and routine practices of their everyday lives (Gutiérrez & Rogoff, 2003).

These are tool-rich environments that make use of a range of mediational means, including students' full linguistic toolkits, to promote deep learning. In these contexts, the students' home language is an unmarked language and is key to an education with transformative potential. Within this framework, literacy is conceptualized as a sociocritical literacy that works to decenter traditional discourses, languages, ideologies, texts, and social practices and utilizes the multimodalities of human expression to extend students' social semiotic toolkits.

A sociocritical literacy is a historicizing literacy that promotes expansive learning (Engeström, 1987) through an understanding of one's own history in ways that reframes and remediates the past so that it becomes a resource for the present and future (Gutiérrez, 2007). Augmented by the study of social theory and embodied learning through *teatro del oprimido* (theatre of the oppressed) in which participants' histories are reframed through remembering and reclaiming an historicized past, a sociocritical literacy serves as a powerful tool for mediating learning in current educational activity, as well as remediating previous educational experiences.[5] Within this framework, students read, write, and discuss rigorous but highly relevant texts available in both Spanish and English. Since deep learning and transformative understandings are the object of a sociocritical literacy, students and instructional staff draw freely from and use English, Spanish, and hybrid language practices to make meaning. In our work, a sociocritical literacy works toward the development of a toolkit that serves to promote a robust literacy (including academic literacy), college-going trajectories, and new sensibilities for future individual and collective action around achieving social justice for nondominant communities—a historicized social justice organized around issues of equity and the standpoint of nondominant communities.

Privileging Equity: Our Miner's Canary

I recognize that successful design experiments like the programs in which I have spent a good deal of my academic life are counterspaces and insufficient to ensure that issues of equity, linguistic and otherwise, remain in the forefront. Toward this end, I propose a radically different accountability apparatus that privileges equity and serves as our miner's canary and works against totalizing, color-blind, and reductive educational paradigms and policies. Like the miner's canary (Guinier & Torres, 2002) that detects the presence of poisonous gases in the mine shaft, a robust equity framework with appropriate indicators will help detect policies and practices that fail nondominant students.

There is an urgent need for new forms of surveillance in educational arenas. Although current educational reform policies are replete with the discourse of access and equality as the central rationale for the development and implementation of new practices, attention to equity drops out early in the instantiation of reform interventions. In many ways, this should come as no surprise if we examine the assumptions, ideologies, and constructs at work in government policies and educational institutions. For example, how do we avoid the deficit framework if we ignore issues of power and inequity and use the performance/achievement gap between students from nondominant and dominant groups as the rationale and justification for reorganizing our schools for implementing new policies? If this is our starting point, what are the possibilities for a new vision of education?

We are living in a paradigm constructed for us. Thus, the development of an equity framework must be constructed from the standpoint of nondominant communities. Such a framework calls for the reframing of the totalizing Black/White paradigm that has resisted alternative frameworks and has defined our nation's history—a framework that imposes a Black essentialism and standpoint on African descent peoples. Instead, I envision a framework of inclusion, a movement toward a theory that accounts for the intersectionality of race, class, gender, and culture and that allows for a strategic essentialism defined by nondominant communities themselves. This shift however needs to occur in terms of strategy, in partnership with other nondominant groups to ensure that no group bleaches out another group. In short, this is not simply an inclusionary framework; rather it must include the various standpoints and histories of nondominant communities to begin to understand how equity is defined across and within communities.

Neither is it a form of multiculturalism, and instead calls for a comprehensive analysis and understanding of the interactive, mutually constitutive relationship among these social categories of race, class, gender, and cultural community. In this way, we can begin to understand, as Hancock (2005) argues, "the way in which race (and/or ethnicity) and gender (or other relevant identity categories) play a salient role in the shaping of political institutions, political actors, and the relationships between institutions and actors"

(p. 76). Here we can begin to redefine the political landscape that imposes strict boundaries between "us" and "them." Within this new framework, intracategory injustices, including the injustices around language, as well as the regularity and variability within cultural communities are acknowledged and incorporated into our analyses (Gutiérrez & Rogoff, 2003; Hancock, 2005).

What I propose here is not new. As Hancock (2005) and Wolfenstein (2006) have pointed out, the intellectual history of intersectionality theory is found in the work of W. E. B. Du Bois (1920/1968; 1940/1968; 1920/2003) who argued for the simultaneity of race, class, and, to an extent, gender. Then, as well as now, his work provides insight into the many facets of injustice and the need for strategic action across cultural communities.

The Equity Trail

The current educational system is founded on inequality and so ensuring equity requires institutionalizing social justice into the structures of accountability. Equity trails, like the miner's canary, can monitor and guide our policies and practices. This form of accountability would trace how equity has been conceptualized and addressed from multiple vantage points, from inception, implementation, to outcome. In addition, equity indices would make visible the social and cognitive consequences of new policies and practices; such indices would be congruent with high expectations for achievement, rich and rigorous learning practices, and respectful learning communities that aim for cultural amplification.

From an equity-oriented perspective, first-order questions of accountability would ask: Are issues of race, ethnicity, language, mobility, culture, and power addressed in the equity framework? Is equity meaningfully addressed in the instructional core? Does the equity framework address within and across subgroup differences in ways that do not monolithically essentialize or define groups such as English Learners and cultural communities? Indeed, demystifying normative conceptions of cultural communities and their language practices is a core activity of monitoring for equity. To help ensure robust and equitable learning environments and practices for nondominant students, we need to institutionalize accountability systems that attend to how equity plays out for all student subgroups. By developing equity trails, policy makers, practitioners, and administrators can be held accountable for inequitable policies and practices. I propose the following guiding questions to help us attend to equity in ways that transform the current policies and practices for nondominant students, especially English Learners:

1. Have issues of equity been part of the conceptualization of the reform?
2. Have appropriate stakeholders been part of the conceptualization and implementation process?
3. Whose notion of equity is reflected in the reform? In other words, who benefits most from the reform? What is the evidence?
4. What are the accountability measures vis-à-vis equity? Are they present throughout the life of the reform?
5. Does the equity framework account for the significant diversity of members of nondominant communities, including English Learners? Of all subgroups? (within and across the subgroup).

There is particular urgency in examining the inequitable schooling of students who are also English Learners. From an equity perspective, opportunity to learn indicators for English Learners would include accounting for (a) students' degree of segregation; (b) rates of mobility; (c) rate of access to high-status knowledge courses; (d) opportunity to acquire college-going behaviors; (e) opportunity for dynamic/multiple pathways or trajectories; (f) opportunity to participate in courses whose practices are organized around meaningful learning and participation; (g) opportunity to have credentialed, well-prepared teachers; and (h) access to powerful literacies.

A robust and historicized equity framework advances a new discourse of accountability—one that is grounded in a humanist vision of society and its institutions where students' right to their own language is realized. But recognizing language and literacy as civil rights is but an important first step toward ensuring a transformative education for students from nondominant communities. Sociocritical literacy will help students mediate the sources of inequality, both historically and presently, locally and globally.

Notes

1. "White innocence" is not about the racial category of Whiteness; rather it is about maintaining the dominant subject position or supremacy. See Gutiérrez (2006) for an elaborated discussion of the concept of "White innocence."

2. I also use the concept of "White innocence" to illustrate how the work of educational researchers can be complicit in maintaining dominance. (See Gutiérrez, 2006 for discussion of this issue.)

3. Ideologies include ideas, representations, beliefs, and constructs that are instantiated in practices (Gal, 1992, as cited in Razfar, 2005).

4. Consider the "accented" language of Arnold Schwarzenegger and Henry Kissinger, or the garbled syntax of President Bush as examples of exceptions made to those in power and from dominant communities.

5. The work of Manuel Espinoza and Hector Alvarez among many others should be acknowledged here for their instrumental role in developing *Teatro* and the Social Science components of these projects.

References

Badillo, H. (2006). *One nation, one standard: An ex-Liberal on how Hispanics can succeed just like other immigrant groups.* New York: Sentinel.

Biko, S. (1978). *I write what I like: A selection of his writings.* New Aelred Stubbs (Ed.). London: Bowerdean.

Committee on CCC Language Statement. (1975). Students' right to their own language. *College English, 3*(6), 709–726.

Crawford, J. (1996). Anatomy of the English only movement: Social and ideological sources of language restrictionism in the United States. Paper presented at a Conference on Language Legislation and Linguistic Rights, University of Illinois at Urbana-Champaign, March 21.

Crosland, K. (2004). Colorblind desegregation: Race neutral remedies as the new "equal opportunity." Paper presented at the annual meeting of the American Educational Research Association, San Diego, California.

Crowther, J., Hamilton, M., & Tett, L. (2001). *Powerful Literacies.* Leicester, UK: National Institute of Adult Continuing Education (NIACE).

Du Bois, W. E. B. (1920/1968). *The souls of black folk.* New York: Johnson Reprint Company.

Du Bois, W. E. B. (1920/2003). *Darkwater: Voices from behind the Veil.* New York: Prometheus Books.

Du Bois, W. E. B. (1940/1968). *Dusk of dawn: An essay towards and autobiography of a race concept.* New York: Schocken Books.

Engeström, Y. (1987). *Learning by expanding: An activity-theoretic approach to developmental research.* Helsinki, Finland: Orienta-Konsultit.

Engeström, Y. (2003). The horizontal dimension of expansive learning: Weaving as texture of cognitive trails in the terrain of health care in Helsinki. In F. Achtenhagen & E. G. John (Eds.), *Milestones of vocational and occupational education and training. Volume I: The teaching-learning perspective* (pp. 1–32). Bielefeld, Germany: Bertelsmann.

Freire, P. (1998). *Pedagogy of freedom: Ethics, democracy, and civic courage* (Trans. P. Clarke). Lanham, MD: Rowman & Littlefield.

Gal, S. (1992). Multiplicity and contention among ideologies: A commentary. *Pragmatics, 2*(3), 445–449.

Gotanda, N. (2004). Reflections on Korematsu, brown and white innocence. *Temple Political and Civil Rights Law Review, 13*, 663.

Guinier, L., & Torres, G. (2002). *The miner's canary: Enlisting race, resisting power, transforming democracy.* Cambridge, MA: Harvard University Press.

Gutierrez, K. (2005). Intersubjectivity and grammar in the third space. Scribner Award Lecture. American Educational Research Association. Montreal, CA.

Gutiérrez, K. (2006). White innocence: A framework and methodology for rethinking educational discourse. *International Journal of Learning, 12,* 1–11.

Gutiérrez, K. (2007). Historicizing Literacy. In M. Blackburn & C. Clark (Eds.), *Literacy Research for Political Action* (pp. ix–xiii). New York: Teachers College Press

Gutiérrez, K., & Arzubiaga, A. (under review). Re-imagining community.

Gutiérrez, K., & Jaramillo, N. (2006). Looking for educational equity: The consequences of relying on *Brown.* In A. Ball (Ed.), *With more deliberate speed: Achieving equity and excellence in education—realizing the full potential of* Brown v. Board of Education (pp. 173–189). 2006 Yearbook of the National Society for the Study of Education, 105(2). Malden, MA: Blackwell .

Gutiérrez, K., & Rogoff, B. (2003). Cultural ways of learning: Individual traits or repertoires of practice. *Educational Researcher, 32*(5), 19–25.

Gutiérrez, K., Asato, J., Pacheco, M., Moll, L., Olson, K., Horng, E., et al. (2002). "Sounding American": The consequences of new reforms on English language learners. *Reading Research Quarterly.* 37(3), 328–343.

Hamilton, M. (1997). Keeping alive alternative visions. In J. P. Hautecoeur, (Ed.). *Alpha 97: Basic Education and Institutional Environments.* Hamburg: UNESCO Institute for Education.

Hancock, A. M. (2005). W.E.B. Du Bois: Intellectual forefather of intersectionality? *Souls,* 7(3–4), 74–84.

Kroscrity, P. (2004). Language ideologies. In Duranti, A. (Ed.), *In companion to linguistic anthropology.* Malden, MA: Basil Blackwell.

O'Reilly, B. (2006). http://www.billoreilly.com/culturewarrior. Retrieved December 19, 2006, from http://www.billoreilly.com

Ochs, E., & Scheffelin, B. (1989). Language has a heart. *The pragmatics of affect, special issue of text,* 9(1), 7–25.

Razfar, A. (2005). Language ideologies in practice: Repair and classroom discourse. *Linguistics in Education, 16,* 404–424.

Rumbaut, R. (2006). The making of a people. In M. Tienda & F. Mitchell (Eds.), *Hispanics and the future of America. Panel on Hispanics in the United States. Committee on Population, Division of Behavioral and Social Sciences and Education* (pp. 16–65). Washington, DC: National Academies Press.

Street, B. (1995). *Social literacies: Critical approaches to literacy in development, ethnography, and education.* London: Longman.

Wolfenstein, E. V. (1993). *Psychoanalytic-Marxism: Groundwork.* New York & London: Gilford Press.

Wolfenstein, V. (2006, May). Personal communication. University of California, Los Angeles.

INDEX

Studies in the Postmodern Theory of Education

General Editors
Joe L. Kincheloe & Shirley R. Steinberg

Counterpoints publishes the most compelling and imaginative books being written in education today. Grounded on the theoretical advances in criticalism, feminism, and postmodernism in the last two decades of the twentieth century, Counterpoints engages the meaning of these innovations in various forms of educational expression. Committed to the proposition that theoretical literature should be accessible to a variety of audiences, the series insists that its authors avoid esoteric and jargonistic languages that transform educational scholarship into an elite discourse for the initiated. Scholarly work matters only to the degree it affects consciousness and practice at multiple sites. Counterpoints' editorial policy is based on these principles and the ability of scholars to break new ground, to open new conversations, to go where educators have never gone before.

For additional information about this series or for the submission of manuscripts, please contact:

Joe L. Kincheloe & Shirley R. Steinberg
c/o Peter Lang Publishing, Inc.
29 Broadway, 18th floor
New York, New York 10006

To order other books in this series, please contact our Customer Service Department:

(800) 770-LANG (within the U.S.)
(212) 647-7706 (outside the U.S.)
(212) 647-7707 FAX

Or browse online by series:
www.peterlang.com